Triple-Portrait of a Countertenor

Maxine Handy

Copyright © Maxine Handy 2010
First published in 2010 by Lulu
Revised edition in 2011 by Lulu

Distributed by Lulu

The right of Maxine Handy to be identified as the author of the work has been asserted herein in accordance with the Copyright, Designs and Patents Act 1988.

All rights reserved. This book is sold subject to the condition that it shall not, by way of trade or otherwise, be lent, resold, hired out or otherwise circulated without the publisher's prior consent in any form of binding or cover other than that in which it is published and without a similar condition including this condition being imposed on the subsequent purchaser

British Library Cataloguing in Publication Data
A catalogue record for this book is available from the British Library

ISBN 978-1-4466-5344-9

Author Profile

Maxine Handy was born next to a wood in Kent, and had a view of the River Thames from her bedroom window. However, she spent her formative years in a small village beneath a wood (Birchanger) on the Herts/Essex border. From there she attended school in antique Saffron Walden where she joined the choir, giving performances of works by Benjamin Britten. Lucky enough to encounter an inspirational English teacher she won many prizes before reading English Language and Literature at the University of Leeds, completing a dissertation on Henry James' short stories of the literary life for her MA. University also gave her an opportunity to study Classical Civilisation and enter the elite seductive atmosphere of the Greek Department. She is also increasingly fascinated by, and drawn to Jewish history, culture, and literature. The author now lives in a tiny village in rural Cheshire, enjoying writing, countertenors, and the company of her two beloved cats and two adult children. She visits mainland Greece and Italy at every opportunity. Having published *The Life of Bosworth – A Cat* in 2007, described by Julian Clary as 'A charming and surprising read'. Maxine is now working on the novelisation of a countertenor memoir, to be published next year.

Also by Maxine Handy

The Life of Bosworth
A Cat

Published by Maniot Books 2007

The Wishing-Well and Other Fantasies

Published by Lulu, 2010

Burning in Blueness
The Dark-light of a Countertenor

Published by Lulu, 2010

To

The Male High Voice

'something unnatural perfected until it sounds natural'

James Bowman

'For I had found the pearl
beyond price and would
be with Him Eternally.'

The Gnostic Gospel of Thomas

Triple Portrait of a Countertenor

Contents

1	Meditation	1
2	War Baby – a Fenland Flame	5
3	Triple-Portrait:	
	a) Notes on a Countertenor 1990-2000, The Story of a Masterpiece	21
	b) Second Study of James Bowman: Britten's Chosen Countertenor	65
	c) Addenda:	
	Reflections on a Distant Artist	87
	Afterword	102
	Coda	107
4	Discography	109

Meditation

James Bowman 1968

'For where your treasure is, there will your heart be also.' You are a devotee of a world-renowned singer; you attend all his concerts and own every recording by him. After a decade of listening to this unique artist the time has come to take the next step, away from the public domain and into a more beautiful and personal realm. Your chosen Countertenor has an esoteric following so your approach must be singular. In the words of Milton, whose poetry he sings, you must come to him 'with an individual kiss'. Begin by offering what you know most intimately - letters, books, and flowers, given in homage to his last English performance of Britten's *A Midsummer Night's Dream*. Send your gifts to him at Sadler's Wells Opera House where he is singing the role of Oberon, the fairy king. Like the dark-light tones he creates, your exquisite bouquet must be sensuous yet austere, two colours only in juxtaposition. Yellow roses burning in blueness are the perfect choice; you are the colour of sunlight and he is the lovely blue.

One day in the future he will see and acknowledge the mediaeval mysticism within your affinity; he will call you 'a living flame'. Use your knowledge of the ancient Greeks to capture his interest and communicate an empathy. Pindar's final pythian Ode will bewitch him as he sees himself exalted, adored, and mirrored in the words. With your beautiful Cross burgundy and gold fountain-pen write him a letter on handmade paper telling him the origin of your obsession. The apotheosis took place on 28th May 1972 when you heard his recital 'Songs for 3 Voices', broadcast live by Radio 3 from the National Gallery, London. The concert was in aid of the Save the Titian fund, a successful campaign to retain the Old Master painting *The Death of Actaeon*. At this truly remarkable concert your singer performed with Benjamin Britten and Peter Pears; he remembered the event as the musical highlight of his career. How strange that this 1972 Song recital was a life-changing experience for both the countertenor making 'the most wonderful noise in the universe', according to his friend and colleague David Munrow, and his ardent listener in Meanwood, Leeds, who at the time was writing her dissertation on Henry James.

Your letter to Sadler's Wells should coincide with his first night performance in the *Dream*; it will explain to him that you intend to be present at three of his five performances. Each time you make the long journey to London and back in a single day, you travel far, very far, to see him. This reminds him that when he was a lonely young chorister at Ely Cathedral, sent away from his home in Newcastle, his mother never visited him because it was 'too far, too far away'. In your very first letter you call him your 'fenland flame', the 'King of Shadows' for you know that Oberon is his *alter ego*. You use the sublime Pindar quotation to inscribe your first gift of Henry James' selected letters. The great singer responds to you with a card; it includes his home address and telephone number. He invites you to phone and receive his engagement list. The approach is tentative but you are beginning to win his trust; he finds it very difficult to trust people.

Soon you will meet frequently at his recitals and on every occasion he will single you out and sing to you alone, leaving you 'in suspended ecstasy until the next time,' and telling you that 'love for a voice is a deeply personal thing, a very beautiful and personal thing.' In his battered old music case are your cards which he brings along to his performances; he often uses your suggested piece for his encore. Your morning flowers brighten his darkness, especially at Easter. In later years you commission a SCENA for his 50th birthday celebration, and you write a memoir documenting your unique and beautiful relationship as artist and audience. When the green-lighted time has come to say goodbye to the veteran countertenor, the living legend, then do so with a loving caress and a charming gesture, knowing that seen through your eyes he has achieved artistic immortality. Remember that your decade of almost daily letters, an aria with diverse variations, will one day be a part of your singer's legacy, to be made into a book and left after his lifetime. He has promised to front-cover it with Leonardo da Vinci's *The Virgin of the Rocks* in remembrance of your vision in which, seated beside you during a concert interval, he metamorphosed into Leonardo's Masterpiece. He described his bass-baritone speaking voice as the cavern in which his alto voice resonates, 'something unnatural perfected until it sounds natural'.

War Baby – A Fenland Flame

Fenland dyke

It was November 1941, a time of austerity, rationing, danger and strict class divisions. War had broken out in the summer of 1939. His birth took place in Oxford, shortly after All Souls Day – that sombre memorial to the dead that is related to ancestor worship of which Geoffrey Hill, the new Oxford professor of poetry would approve. November is the darkest month, especially in wartime. For the French, it is marked by chrysanthemums; the flowers of dissolution and decay are placed everywhere. France was to become a second home for the baby born on November 6th, and to have a seminal effect on his adult life and triumphant career. As a young singer he would dazzle those fortunate enough to encounter him in the 1960s and 70s, but in childhood his life was difficult.

Baby James Thomas arrived into conflict – parental, national and international. England was at war and there were similar divisions within his home. By the time James was four years old his parents had divorced, although his country was now at peace. The marriage of his parents had been disastrously unhappy and had ended badly. Things were subsequently very hard for James' mother. She found herself with two young boys and no husband. Her first-born son was equable and relatively untroubled by the disastrous situation at home, but her second child, James Thomas, was a strange boy, impossible to fathom. He had always seemed problematic, given to terrible tantrums. Charles was outgoing, intelligent and straightforward, but his brooding younger brother was dreamy, clumsy, and often difficult. Now that he was fatherless at such an early age, how would she cope, and make a successful man of him, she mused.

One solution was to take advantage of his obvious gift for singing. She had not expected him to have a special talent, but he surprised her by his bond with music. It offered a sanctuary into which he could happily withdraw. Indeed, it seemed to James' mother that the identity of her infant boy was inseparable from that of words in music. To these he always listened; to all else he was indifferent. Certainly he rarely attended to anything his mother said to him, and she found this withdrawal from her infuriating.

However, his autocratic and ambitious mother quickly realised that her son's sole talent might be turned to advantage, the outcome of which would be beneficial to them both. James' unexpected gift, if nurtured by the right people and institutions, could liberate them both from their uneasy relationship and impoverished circumstances. The post-war years suddenly looked less dark to her. For James, they were to be a long period of isolation without privacy, the worst imaginable combination and certain to inflict lasting damage. His home for a decade was to be a cold cathedral, intensifying his longing for admission to the warmth and intimacy of another soul.

The unprotected journeying boy set out for the desolate Cambridgeshire fens at the age of nine, in Festival of Britain year – that vulgar show of enterprise and national unity despised by Winston Churchill. Of exalted Anglo-Irish lineage and singular good looks, he ran the risk of becoming the dormitory beauty boy at the Cathedral Choir School. His mother believed that he had taken his first step towards the elite arena which she envisaged for his adult life. To this end, she was wholly supportive, unlike his totally uninterested, absent father. James' undoubted talent, if carefully nurtured, might serve a useful purpose. His mother had decided to be ruthless in her objective; it was for the good of her son that she be so. A brisk goodbye and his mother disappeared.

The Cathedral was overwhelmingly vast to a small boy. The school had a horrible smell and the freezing dormitory resembled a stark hospital ward. The years ahead in this remote, monastic place seemed unbearably endless. When he looked at the others marooned here, tears welled up and his cheeks flushed in anger. He thought of the nearby river and longed to escape like his hero Tom, the poor little chimney-sweep in *The Water Babies*, his favourite book. At home in the far-off North-East of England lay the book, hidden away in a bedside drawer. It was an illustrated version and he had never tired of gazing at the picture on the cover, which depicted Tom as he prepared to dive into the freezing Arctic waters on his mission to find benign old Mother Carey.

The haunting image was one of loneliness, courage, endurance and yearning. The outcast little boy has only the crying gulls and his small dog for company. Poor Tom shivers and hesitates as he looks out across the endless, turbulent ocean. Many dangers and adventures await him beneath the waves, but the sea also offers him transformation and freedom.

As young James tried to comfort himself with thoughts of Charles Kingsley's wonderful story, he wondered if rescue would ever come to him. He had been abandoned in a dark, remote place. Little did he realise that within two decades he would be propelled to world fame by a composer who had also loved Kingsley's *The Water Babies* in his own Suffolk childhood, and been changed by his reading of it. The book was an inspirational thread running through their lives; one day it would unite the great composer with his chosen countertenor muse, James. The lost boy, painfully adjusting and adapting to his fenland vault was destined for musical glory, as beloved and god. Artistic immortality would replace human happiness.

Genius had undoubtedly accompanied him as he came out of his mother's womb, but he had to work incredibly hard to nurture his gift. He had been singing since infancy and entered his local Cathedral choir at the age of four, but he truly found his voice and repertoire during his decade at Ely. It was there that he developed the instrument of his soul. Those years of discipline as a chorister would ultimately lead him to the Oxford choirs and to Sir Peter Pears, his sometime mentor and singing teacher, who taking him by the hand on the lawn of the Red House, Aldeburgh, and running with him towards the rehearsal room where Benjamin Britten awaited them, would change his life forever.

This glorious future lay far away from the agony of James' first night in the juniors' school dormitory. The atmosphere was forbidding; the stony silence frequently interrupted by the weeping of homesick young boys, packed off just like him. Sending children away to a single-sex exile, where bullying and beatings were routine, was an English disease at this time. No-one questioned an educational system for young males which favoured emotional deprivation, love-withdrawal, and often sadistic control by Masters at the school. Even sexual abuse was concealed and tolerated as almost a necessary rite-of-passage, which would ultimately lead to a privileged existence amidst important contacts for adult life. James himself was soon exposed to such unwanted attention. Like Greek pederasty in the ancient world, such an initiation was viewed as good preparation for the nepotism of Oxford University, one's ultimate goal and probable destination. As James rose to singing the alto line as a senior, he was increasingly exposed to sexual predators within the lay-clerk community. The boys were warned never to be alone with one such man, a notorious abuser who enticed the seniors into his study. A fatherless adolescent in crisis was especially vulnerable to this twisted interest and attention. And as it was offered with the promise of musical advancement, the gifted boy might misunderstand the intentions beneath the innocent-seeming disguise. In all such cases, it was the young victim who would feel lifelong guilt, mingled with revulsion or possible confused attraction, for he would be made to believe that he was responsible for having seduced the older man. As James grew more moody, discontented, vocally brilliant, and arrestingly handsome, he was increasingly cast in the role of grudging tempter. Only in the inspiration and austerely beautiful Lady Chapel did he feel loved and empathetic. In the fens he cultivated the humour of the observer and outsider. His gift for irony and ambiguity was remarkable, whilst his sense of the pompous and absurd gave rise to wickedly funny and witty comments which slow recipients failed to grasp. Also, through his art he could creatively opt out of the human situation and achieve an aesthetic renunciation of the dark world surrounding him.

By the time that he was 16, James was ready to sing with the other male altos in the now-famous Cathedral Choir, but also advanced enough to make his debut as a soloist with Purcell's *Here the Deities Approve*.

Under the tutelage of the brilliant and unique choirmaster, Michael Howard, and his assistant organist, Dr Arthur Wills, James had developed a sensational sound of great power and beauty, but the loss of his boy-soprano voice had occurred in traumatic circumstances. Years later, he would say that his voice changed gradually and underwent a natural transition, especially as Howard encouraged his boys to use falsetto, but on other occasions, James would tell a story of his miserable time in the school sanatorium. Confined there because of a severe throat infection, he said that when he at last came out of the place, his voice had broken. As his mother lived so far away, she seldom or never visited him, not even during his illness. This enforced separation, justified to him by his distant mother living too far away to make the journey to his school, must have left him heartbroken and grudge-bearing. Little wonder that, after his time at Oxford University, he was temporarily semi-estranged from his family.

However, luck was on his side on the occasion of his amazing early debut as a professional soloist in front of a large, paying audience. James loved to show off, and here he was singing countertenor in the public domain! It excited and delighted him to be unexpectedly giving a performance of a wonderful Purcell song, the words of which were deeply prophetic. In future years James would often crown a special occasion by singing this song, an emblem of his career:

'Here the deities approve,
The god of Music and of Love.
All the talents they have lent you,
All the blessings they have sent you,
Pleas'd to see what they bestow,
Live and thrive so well below.'

On that first occasion in 1957, the solo was to have been performed by an alto from the visiting Cambridge College Choir, but he had been indisposed so James had substituted at the last minute. When, in future years, he applied for a choral scholarship at King's College, he was unsuccessful. The

University of Cambridge would later acknowledge their mistake in missing such an opportunity to nurture James' amazing talent, but by then he was world-renowned and Cambridge often invited him to perform as a soloist with their best choirs, including those of King's Trinity and St John's.

He only got into Oxford because of his voice. When, at interview, he modestly mentioned his academic limitations but asked to be allowed to sing to the panel of men, he was welcomed to the University on a choral scholarship. Nominally, he was reading modern history but, in reality, he spent all his time singing with the choirs of New College and nearby Christ Church Cathedral. His genius was identified at once by another outstanding musician and unusual human being, the great David Munrow. He knew immediately that this was the voice he had been searching for, instrumental in tone and with the power and resonance of a clarion call. David described it as 'the most wonderful noise in the universe'.

Imprisoned during childhood in a dream/nightmare, and bored by Oxford and the drudgery of prep-school teaching, James was now given life-changing opportunities. He could travel the world, work with the very best pioneers in early music, and inspire the creation of new repertoire written specifically for his voice. One of his greatest-ever recitals was given on May 28th 1972 at the National Gallery in London. Its title was *Songs for Three Voices*, performed in aid of the 'Save the Titian' fund. The other singers were the baritone John Shirley-Quirk and the tenor Peter Pears, with Benjamin Britten accompanying on the piano. Included in the programme were Britten's Canticles II and IV and his Purcell realisation *Sweeter than Roses*. The 30-year-old countertenor was a dedicatee of Canticle IV, and Britten's *Sweeter than Roses*, inspired by the aria *I know a Bank* from the *Dream*, was transposed especially for him. He was to remember this concert as a highlight of his entire career, a Henry Jamesian apotheosis:

'To do a concert with Benjamin Britten and Peter Pears was a rare, and wonderful, irreplaceable experience, and I'll never forget it ... it was one of the great moments in my musical life. I remember it very well ... I can remember the whole occasion. I mean it was a dream come true –'

Listening spellbound to this 28th May 1972 performance was a young student at the University of Leeds; she was working on her dissertation on Henry James. The song, originally composed for Peter Pears, was like an encounter with a living spirit, 'a love-philtre or fear-philtre, which fixes for the senses their supreme symbol of the fair or the strange.' The application of this unique countertenor Tessitura worked its dramatic magic on every syllable. For James, singing high perpetually at approximately one octave above his speaking voice was a technical challenge, not a psychological one. He was entirely comfortable with his chosen voice, an upward extension of his boy-treble.

A personal meeting between the singer and his devoted admirer did not take place until a further two decades, on September 19th 1992. After 20 years of adoration, and almost two years of correspondence, flowers and telephone conversations, she was, at last, introduced to him at a recital. He was singing lute songs with the great and unique Robert Spencer at Hinckley Music Club, where he was then President.

Their empathy was immediate and she was soon receiving his personal recital list and attending almost all his concerts in England. On every occasion, he singled her out to sing to, making his music personal and beautiful:

'Show me where you're sitting and I'll open my mouth very wide and sing to you ... my live performances should leave you in suspended ecstasy, waiting for the next time ... They live and then die like a flower, but there should never be any sense of anti-climax.'

She gave him an inscribed book to commemorate each of his special occasions, and he soon acquired a large *Henry*

James Library given in his honour. In addition, he received almost daily letters from her and exquisite flowers, usually yellow in blue, or blue and white in austere juxtaposition. To celebrate his 50th birthday, his devotee commissioned a scena for solo countertenor and string quartet, written by his friend and former teacher, the organist; Arthur Wills. It was a setting of Robert Browning's poem *A Toccata of Galuppi's*, and received its first performance at Hinckley, where David Munrow had once been the President of the Music Club.

Whilst seated close beside him during the interval, after his world-premier performance of Geoffrey Burgon's *Merciless Beauty* at High Wycombe's flint church, she had a vision in which he was transformed into Leonardo da Vinci's beautiful painting *The Virgin of the Rocks*. Mary is depicted in a cool, watery wilderness, seated beside the archangel Gabriel, whilst her hand rests protectively on the shoulder of the infant John the Baptist who is blessed by the Christ-child. The figure of the Virgin emerges from the shadowed sea-cave through chiaroscuro as we move from darkness into light. It is the sanctuary where each soul waits for its interpreter, the gloomy cavern containing the miraculous thing within.

She saw something in her beloved artist that others had never seen. He recognised at once the truth of her vision. 'You see what I am! Seen through your eyes, I *am* Leonardo's beautiful *Virgin of the Rocks*.' A few years later, in a discussion on Radio 3, he described his low-baritone speaking voice as a cavern in which his alto voice resonates. There was also a strong identification with the infant Christ and his mother, as having only a father in heaven, God the creator. And in Greek mythology caves are often points of access to the underworld, the Elysian fields of the heroes in an afterlife, or even to the gods themselves. Thus they are places of transformation connected to other states of being. In Leonardo's *Virgin of the Rocks*. the interplay of the natural setting and the devotional image disclosed within, is scenery fit for a great man of music. The poet Rilke, who was fascinated by the classical world, said that the creative artist's deepest experience was'... as though a woman had taken a seat within him.'

In his wonderful middle-years, James, the countertenor, had found his perfect audience of one with whom he felt a deep link via the ancient Greeks. The very first flowers she had sent him, to honour his five performances of Britten's *Dream* at Sadler's Wells, were accompanied by a quotation from Pindar's final ode written in the fifth century BC He loved the quote so much that he immediately pinned it up in his kitchen:

'Creatures of a day. What are we, what are we not? The dream of a shadow is man, but when god-given radiance comes; there is a shining light and a sweet time for men.'

He appreciated the Greek love of beauty and understanding of light and darkness, the realms of the spirit and the flesh which were difficult to reconcile. This chasm between the spirit and the senses is also expressed by the modern Greek writer Nikos Kazantzakis; James' passionate admirer often quoted from him in her letters: 'Within me are the dark immemorial forces of the Evil one ... within me too are the luminous forces – and my soul is the arena where these two armies have clashed and met. The anguish has been intense. I loved my body and did not want it to perish; I loved my soul and did not want it to decay.'

James understood this eternal sense of conflict; it was found within the dark-light tones of his own voice and his *alter ego*, Oberon. The role of King of Shadows in Britten's opera, *A Midsummer Night's Dream*, is one of pure libido, beyond gender. When it was performed by James, Britten said that he had vindicated his choice of a countertenor in this role. And when Peter Hall directed him as Oberon, he remarked that this singer had 'lust written all over his lower register'. As so often in Britten's chamber operas, there is a possibility of resolving dissent and opposition, but then it all goes wrong and conflict returns.

James regarded his sweet and kind admirer as 'a pearl amongst swine', and told her how grateful he was and that he must endeavour to deserve her devotion. 'I'm loved and adored,' he said. 'Don't stop adoring me.' She had opened his eyes to books and a unique interpretation of his work. Like Minny Temple for Henry James, she felt 'a love as intense as faith; passing through the senses into mystery.'

He kept all her letters because they were so very interesting and beautiful. One day when perhaps his career might come to an end, he intended to compile a book from her letters, to be left after his lifetime. He would edit her decade of private correspondence and the book cover was to be Leonardo's *The Virgin of the Rocks*, his fine-art memorial. Her only other love was the voice of Peter Pears who had been a lifelong influence on his own art. Like him, she loathed populism and the plebeian, and like David Munrow, his long lost friend, she limelighted his voice alone.

Amidst his kind and charming appreciation of all that she had given him in the 10 years of contact, he had also given her a warning not to become too obsessed. Through no fault of his own, his friends and close collaborators sometimes became 'overly fond', falling in love with the beauty of his voice, and developing a destructive obsession which was not his fault. He had made his music intensely personal for her, saying, 'I don't care about the world, not while I still have you.' On many occasions, she had brightened his darkness and brooding gloom with the gift of flowers. She was the colour of sunlight and he the lovely blue. He had a surprising fear of being laughed at in unsympathetic venues, or simply of being misunderstood or not appreciated. Like all the greatest artists, he was sometimes insecure, even mildly paranoid. He had always resisted any idea of a conventional biography; it simply did not interest him. And he did not want people 'fingering' his private life; his true biography lay in the huge number of recordings he had made. He had paid tribute to his highly perceptive and adoring friend by his promise to use her correspondence to him as part of his eventual legacy to the world.

James knew that he had been damaged in childhood by the monastic authoritarian, single-sex environment of Ely Cathedral Choir School – an environment almost totally devoid of women. The great pain of separation at such an early age had remained with him for years, especially before going to sleep or when he was tidying his things. It was so cold in the fens in winter that the river often froze, all the way to Cambridge. Like the poet John Clare in Epping Forest, he had felt homeless at home and longed to escape. A tragic drowning in the river had occurred whilst he was at the school; one boy who had never returned.

His gratitude to his devoted friend who frequently travelled so very, very far to see him in performance, and came such a long, long way from her prime venues in London, contrasted with his sense of betrayal by his own mother. Once he was adult, his mother probably chose to ignore as unreal his imperfections and, instead, focus on his overwhelming achievements. He remembered that when his letter had arrived from Benjamin Britten informing him of his successful audition for the role of Oberon, the role that would propel him to fame, he had been on holiday in the Italian Lakes and his mother had opened the letter. James had been furious with her but repressed his anger. But she had wounded him. All these inner tensions were now in the public domain, but he sounded a further warning note to his literary friend in private, following a winter recital in Ilkley: 'My work is the most important thing in my life – it comes before everything. I cannot return others' feelings for me.' As she looked intently up at him, she wondered if his beautiful expressive eyes were those of his mother, which had been handed down to him like ancestral jewels. On this occasion in Yorkshire, they said goodbye to one another with a warm, very English handshake in the brilliant moonlight.

Travelling home by train that night, it occurred to her that her friend's genius was likely to possess the imagination of great musicians with a confused identity – people in conflict such as the late David Munrow, and Robert King, who had worshipped the countertenor since 1972 when he had performed alongside him as a boy-treble and realised his dream of working with him as an adult. Like Peter Hall's description of the enchanted forest in the *Dream*, James was 'a dangerous place of strange alterations', and he must always be in control of his anarchic wood, otherwise he went mad. Unsurprisingly, he was always 'getting rid of people', as he coldly put it.

After each decade, he would become restless and bored, and search for new challenges and different directions. The longevity of his singing voice was simply amazing; it was truly god-given. With David Munrow, he had explored a repertoire of largely medieval music, although his final recording with the early music consort had been of Monteverdi and his contemporaries. Having made his debut in the *Dream* at the age of 26, his rise had been meteoric. But, in 1976, he suffered a double tragedy; David died by his own hand in Chesham Bois and Britten failed to recover from a serious heart operation. Both men would have had so much more to offer him in the future. Munrow's interest in baroque music would have developed and centred on James, the focus of his entire ensemble, and Britten was writing a lute-song cycle for him and also intended to re-write the *Dream* to make the part of Oberon more complex, interesting, and challenging for his voice.

After the four-year vocal crisis which followed David's suicide, his 1981 Glyndebourne *Dream* restored his confidence, as did his fruitful 10-year collaboration with

Robert King and his consort. King himself is now, in 2010, recovering his own career after a tragic downfall some few years ago. And the greatest countertenor in the world continues to develop marvellous contemporary repertoire for the voice; much of the music he commissions himself. He has now cut back on his exhausting international programme, but still performs regularly in France, his second home for so many years. Having been appointed CBE in 1997 for services to music, he has also returned to singing on Sundays as a Gentleman of the Chapel Royal, in the personal service of the Queen.

James' devoted admirer of a decade felt deeply grateful for the privilege of having known such a man and artist for more than a decade. She had blessed him with a written portrait of his genius, and she often heard her own words when he was subsequently in discussion on Radio 3. In 1998 she had given him an inscribed copy of Henry James' *The Story of a Masterpiece*. 'It's so perfectly true,' she wrote, 'that as you slowly fade and your voice darkens with age like the tones of the "Old Master", you become an ever more beautiful Masterpiece.'

He loved this idea and subsequently referred to himself in interview with Brian Kay, as 'an old Masterpiece hanging there'. James was also indebted to her for his beautiful library, which included almost everything by the Auschwitz survivor Primo Levi, including his poetry collection *Ad Ora Incerta*. When he went to Paris for his final tour of the *Dream* he took her library with him. And many years later, he commissioned a work from the composer Ari Frankel, which was inspired by his interest in Levi. It is a marvellous piece with the title *Wiping Ceramic Tiles*. His 2004 recording *Songs for Ariel* is a musical autobiography, 'each track a voyage through a world all its own'. When he revisits his earlier repertoire, the effect is profoundly moving and deeply thrilling.

He describes his voice as something unnatural, perfected until it sounds natural. A former lay-clerk at his boyhood Cathedral remembered him there at the age of eighteen-and-a-half: 'He had phenomenal breath control. He was amazing even then. I don't know when he breathes – I've never seen it.' He also mentioned that James never mentioned his family whilst at school; they seemed not to exist. 'One thought of him as the son of God!' James' later preference for smaller venues arose from his early years in the huge vaulted space of the Cathedral with its boomy acoustic; the boys' voices were trained to accommodate to it. His deep need for warmth and intimacy found expression in lute-song recitals and Handel's Italian Chamber Duets, one of his finest ever recordings of his dear Handel.

Theirs was a musical love-affair made in heaven, in the colours of the rainbow. He almost single-handedly revived Handel's castrato roles and made them central to his specialist heroic repertoire. When he returned to sing with his old Cathedral Choir, James liked to retrace by car his old schoolboy cross-country running route. His experiences at Ely King's School and beyond had left him both social and reclusive. He would have gone mad without his friends, but like Henry James, he possessed the 'solitude of genius'. His aura was one of loneliness. James was always more moon than sun, and after 10 years of ecstatic communion with him, darkness finally fell for his worshipper. At his request, she embraced him, and gave him a goodbye kiss in the foyer of Snape Maltings. He had sung to her for the last time. His programme had been perfect; the *Ten Blake Songs* and a selection of lute songs. It was Easter Monday and outside was the solace of falling snow. The voice she had fallen in love with in May 1972 when he was 30 was not the same as the one she returned to in the late 1980s. It was even more remarkable, complex, and beautiful, having developed greater plangency. But James believed that he was past his very best by the end of 1998, although he would continue to dominate, inspire and dazzle all those he worked with.

Like James, she understood the need for renunciation, and knew that the dislocation of time during 10 years at a forbidding choir school had left its traumatic mark. In the words of Jean Améry, he had been *At the Mind's Limits*, recalling scenes with a painful clarity of vision. For an entire decade she had retained his interest and kindness; wrapping her in the dignity of his art. For, as James had once said to her in private after bestowing a performance: 'Love for a voice is something very personal; it is a deeply personal thing.'

Triple Portrait

James Bowman in his garden

Notes on a Countertenor 1990-2000: The Story of a Masterpiece

In his Notebooks, Leonardo da Vinci records a moment when, standing before the mouth of a Cave 'suddenly two things arose in me…fear of the menacing darkness [and] desire to see if there was any marvellous thing within…'

Like Actaeon gazing at Diana in her grotto, Leonardo saw 'stillness and grace/in the space of one heartbeat/then he saw his own death.' An apotheosis he made visible in *The Virgin of the Rocks*.

This Cave was for the artist a physical place from childhood; a natural landscape of rocks and wreath-like flowers enfolding art and myth. In the watery wilderness where life floats in suspension, the Virgin Mary shelters her infant son and John the Baptist, his prophet and follower. Leonardo's composition an open triangle where man, woman, and consensual angel mingle, sublimed through chiaroscuro. Emerging from the shadows the winged-Gabriel kneels reverently; a messenger from the world I was seeking, far away from ocean storms. To be ultimately admitted perhaps, to the 'warmth and intimacy of another soul', something that the countertenor James Bowman frequently quoted back to me as something that he, too, desperately wanted. Scenery fit for music's very treasure and master:

'The deepest experience of the creative artist is feminine, for it is an experience of conceiving and giving birth...as though a woman had taken a seat within him.'
Rilke

Peter Giles described me as having 'a unique relationship with the countertenor voice', adding that 'It would be a great shame for you both if your friendship ever faltered.' He said that whenever he heard Josquin Desprez *'Déploration sur la mort de Johannes Ockeghem'*, he always thought of me and my devotion to the voice of James Bowman. Peter called Josquin's beautiful lament, 'Max's piece.'

March 2008
A decade of writing – recorded jewels – concluded with a memoir bound in dark-blue cloth with gold-leaf lettering. Edited by Sonia Ribeiro over a period of two years. Now a close friend whom I visit often in Golders Green. Eighty thousand words to honour my long-lost friend, a blue jewel, in a poetic and visitable past. Five copies only for private distribution – signed with my burgundy and gold *Cross Signature* fountain pen, which James held and admired as 'beautiful' when embellishing my *Galuppi* score. Afterwards, carefully returning my pen to its *Mont Blanc* leather case, decorated with a single snowflake.

Devotion, worship, obsession and metamorphosis. Whether *the King of Shadows* recreated or destroyed, I am still uncertain.

- like those who looked into the eyes of Picasso. The man was a paradox, a Dracula. He fed on his devotees and seduced them all. People were happy to be consumed by him. They remember the scrutiny of his amazing eyes; 'they burned...that was God looking at me,' said Sylvette.
Reading my memoir of James *Burning in Blueness*
The Dark-Light of a Countertenor
My mother said 'You write about him as though he is dead, a Henry Jamesian "immortal absence".'

A tripartite structure. Three decades covered by four paintings:
The frontispiece and Introduction:
Leonardo da Vinci *The Virgin of the Rocks*
- for immortality. -
Three fine-art portraits express a changing persona:
The Voice: Ferdinand Bol *Man with a Hawk*
- for bright, youthful beauty.
The Man: Giorgione *Head of a Man*
-for the brooding middle years in conflict and triumph.
The Memory: John Singer Sargent *Henry James, The Master*
- for the slowly fading, darkening tones of an ever more beautiful Masterpiece: *Gloriani*
'A face that was like an open letter in a foreign tongue. With his genius in his eyes, his manners on his lips, his long career behind him and honours and rewards all round.'
Henry James, *The Ambassadors.*

In search of a voice
Zeus split the human race into male and female, but memories of primeval unity linger on. Longing to find the plangent singer, unlike any other. Touching every syllable. A singer with an individual kiss. Lover of his music working at it with precision, discipline, and pride. 'I didn't come out of

my mother's womb like this! I've had to work at it, and take care of my voice', he confided. The physical splendour of his strong upper body, invisible breathing, and agile tongue – all resonate with a light mechanism. The shadow of history resides in his falsetto, 'something unnatural perfected until it sounds natural', as he often described it: 'If I work on placing my speaking voice low, it gives a sort of cavern in which my alto voice can resonate.'

Perhaps it is significant that at the age of sixteen, in London's National Gallery, I first glimpsed Leonardo's sea-cave which anticipated my epiphanies in 1972 and 1997. Leonardo worked on *The Virgin of the Rocks* through an epidemic of bubonic plague: In *Flights of the Mind*, Charles Nicholl writes, 'In Leonardo the mouth of hell has become a scene of serene benediction.' Four years later, the first time I heard James Bowman sing was in a live recital centred on the National Gallery's quest to save Titian's *The Death of Actaeon*. Once again the marvellous and the frightening are interwoven. A place believed to be miraculous and mysterious like Leonardo's cavern or Tytania's bank, or Henry James' *Galerie d'Apollon* in the Louvre, suddenly and unexpectedly becomes dangerous and frightening. Epiphany turns to destruction; a love-philtre is also a fear-philtre 'which fixes forever our sense of the fair and the strange.'

May 28th 1972

Seated upstairs, in love with high places, I was happily researching Henry James and re-reading his late novel *The Wings of the Dove*. Thinking of his dead cousin Minnie Temple, 'a dancing flame of thought', immortalised in the heroine Milly Theale, I looked again at his memoir of her. Through his writing his outlived and precious friend returned from 'death's dateless night'.

Suddenly, I fled my desk and stood at the top of the staircase, listening and running after the sound heard from below: broadcast from the National Gallery, *Songs for Three Voices*. At once I fell in love with the Britten/Purcell *Sweeter than Roses*, here transposed especially for Britten's chosen countertenor. An ice-fire song that had bewitched David Munrow. 'A paradox of chilly fire'. Many years later in 2002 referring to this concert, James said 'I like the *Sweeter than Roses* Ben did with me. I think that's very beautiful. It has a curiously, almost Schubertian charm about it...To do a concert with Benjamin Britten and Peter Pears was a rare, and wonderful irreplaceable experience and I'll never forget it...It was one of the great moments of my musical life...I can remember the whole occasion. I mean it was a dream come true'.

On May 28th 1972, listening in an old stone cottage by a birch wood – it was the musical highlight of my life. The Purcell Song belongs to James alone. I've heard many others attempt it; they have all failed.

1976: The year of the scorching never-ending summer. Both Britten and Munrow died in this same year, unexpectedly and tragically gone for ever. 'It was awful, Maxine, awful...I felt completely rootless,' said James talking softly to me, gently warming up his voice ready to sing to me as he always promised. 'Poor dear David, poor dear darling boy', Marjorie King had said to me at Hinckley, recalling her devastation on the day of his funeral.

1992: As I looked up at my singer and listened to the voice, described by David Munrow as 'the most wonderful noise in the universe', and by me as 'the most beautiful view on earth', I felt for him what Henry James had felt for Minnie Temple: 'a love as intense as faith; passing through the senses into mystery.'

The Dream: Oberon the fairy king – your *alter ego*.

Three times to Sadler's Wells in November: I wanted to see all five performances. 'You are an addict' said the King of Shadows.

Three long train journeys arriving home to my village at dawn. Writing responses to your creation as I travelled through the night.

I gave him a Library which with typical wit, he named after me. A place of sweet withdrawal from the world. 'Life is terrible' he said. 'And yes, death is agony' I replied. Each volume was dated and inscribed to celebrate a special occasion – 'Thank you for your kindness and devotion to me. I'll endeavour to deserve it' he thoughtfully responded. As a mark of particular esteem I gave him a precious first edition of Henry James *Portraits of Places*. He enjoyed travel literature and Henry James' voyaging resembled his own.

To accompany a bouquet of yellow roses in blue welcoming him home from wintry Florence, I enclosed a quotation from the reclusive poet, Emily Dickinson:

'A Voice that Alters – low
And on the Ear can go
Like Let of Snow –
Or shift supreme –
As tone of Realm
On subjects Diadem - '

For James himself is both social and reclusive. The solitude of genius is in conflict with a deep need for company, and an equal aversion to those he distrusts. Although he loves to talk and enjoy 'discourse with intelligent women', he is difficult to engage in serious conversation, preferring to tell amusing anecdotes, and like Oberon, will suddenly disappear. Peter Giles, who first met him in his Ely days, has said that he has never managed to have a proper conversation with him. 'Just when you're thinking *ah! Got him at last*, he walks away from you...' Like Emily Dickinson's *Visitor in Marl*, he 'Caresses – and is gone.'

In that ancient flint church of St Mary's, High Wycombe, I was looking intently at my singer when he suddenly transformed into Leonardo's painting. Seen through my eyes he became *The Virgin of the Rocks*. I told him of the beauty I had seen, and he said at once that my vision of his transformation expressed perfectly his changed-voice, 'a baritone in the morning, a countertenor by night.' The metamorphosis held the enchantment of Oberon's narcotic 'flower of purple dye', his love-juice. James acknowledged that I had taken the trouble to become intimate with his singing voice and repertoire, to understand his place of strange alteration:

'I think we're very alike', he said. 'We have an empathy, Maxine. We have something very beautiful.'

Walking with my mother in the mountains above Lake Garda, I imagined you there in 1960 with Christopher Campling, Chaplain at Ely, and also as a young man waiting and hoping for the life-changing letter from Benjamin Britten. 'This is the man' wrote the composer at your sole audition, your eroticism vindicating his choice of the countertenor voice for the role of *Oberon*. 'Britten and Pears saw something in Bowman that nobody else had seen', said Peter Giles to me at his home in Kent.

High above the mystical blue, Italian Lake of Garda we rested in the heat. My mother lay on some shaded cool stones and briefly slept. As I walked towards the broken iron gates of a distant villa, a black snake rustled past in the golden grass. In this haunted high-noon landscape the imagined music of an invisible countertenor descended, 'wrapping her in the dignity of his art'.

Your *Dream* at Sadler's Wells in 1991, rumoured to be your last in England, coincided with your 50th birthday. I sent your first florists roses, accompanied by the words of Pindar's last pythian Ode. You told me on the telephone that you loved these words as so appropriate to your fairy king, and had pinned them up at once on your kitchen wall:

'Creatures of a day – what are we, what are we not?
The dream of a shadow is man.
But when god-given radiance comes,
There is a shining light for men and a sweet time.'

It was the Greeks of the fifth century BC who first enabled me to enter the singing life of England's greatest countertenor and elite musician. 'O we love the Greeks, don't we Maxine? And we hate weddings.'

My private commission to commemorate James Bowman's 50th birthday is acknowledged by Dr Arthur Wills in his recent memoir, *Full with Wills*. He composed a Scena for solo countertenor and string quartet, a setting of Browning's poem *A Toccata of Galuppi's*. The twenty minute piece explores human mortality in an evocation of music and Venice in the 18th century, a period during which the male high voice was at its zenith. Arthur's scena was contemporary music inspired by the antique – just perfect for James.

The first performance took place at Hinckley, where James Bowman was president of the Music Club; David Munrow had been a predecessor there. I had always felt close to Munrow because, like me, he read English and his love of literature, especially drama, had inspired his love of vocal music. James was undoubtedly his muse as the chosen singer for his early music consort; his instrumental quality was exactly what David was seeking. It continues to ignite James' work today: 'Sometimes I feel I interact more with instrumentalists than with other singers', he said in a recent interview.

From commission to completion took three years; it was finished on my birthday, 26th January. It was strange to reflect that James had given his first public performance as a countertenor soloist, aged sixteen, whilst still at Ely under the guidance of Dr Wills. Your debut piece was Purcell's *Here the Deities Approve*. How prophetic an aria by Britten's musical ancestor.

> 'Here the Deities approve
> The god of Music and of Love;
> All the talents they have lent you,
> All the blessings they have sent you,
> Pleas'd to see what they bestow,
> Live and thrive so well below.'

You have always acknowledged that for most people, 'singing high perpetually is odd', and you were occasionally teased at school, but for you the challenge was purely technical, not psychological. Even as a chorister you were a boy-alto rather than a boy-soprano, and already deeply attached to the countertenor repertoire. You rose above the multitude to fulfil your 'true and ultimate vocation.'

James Bowman was delighted with my commission and wrote to me in praise of Wills' setting of the Browning poem. 'It is a marvellous piece, full of piquancy and harmonic twists. He has cleverly incorporated some of Galuppi's music into it, giving it a Baroque/Contemporary flavour. I hope you are as pleased as I am.'

On the evening of the premiere he thanked me for the beautiful roses received that morning and the marvellous *Scena* of which at my request, he agreed to be the dedicatee. 'Your enthusiasm has born worthwhile fruit. You have given me a major piece of new repertoire for which I am very grateful. Without you none of this would have come about. You Maxine, will have many opportunities to hear this piece...' James and Arthur discussed which venue they preferred for a second performance. Arthur favoured the Wigmore Hall, but James seemed to prefer St John's, Smith

Square for a London premiere. My choice of card for the commission was Odilon Redon's pastel, *Orpheus*.

During the long hot summer preceding the September *Galuppi* you invited me to your *Messiah* at Ely Cathedral. This took place in a week of very long journeys, which enabled me to see you in four live performances. I came to adore your 'Singer's Face' as Janet Baker has termed it; the sense that beauty gives of divinity. It was always there, even in infancy and boyhood, as only recently seen photographs make clear.

At Hampton Court you changed your programme to give me Handel's aria *Verdi Prati* because I loved it so and asked you hopefully if it was included. Like Ruggiero in the garden of Handel's enchantress *Alcina*, I was 'held captive in a kind of dream, by the promise of endless ecstasy.'

Only a few days later you kept your promise, oh so sublimely, of singing to me in the vastness of Ely Cathedral '"He was despised and rejected" will be for you, Maxine'. Instead of singing 'straight down the Nave' you turned to me in the North Transept to give me this aria, even though it was most awkward for you to do so.

Courteously, he introduced me to his old teacher and friend Dr Arthur Wills OBE, and then remained in Ely until the early hours of the morning to work on *A Toccata of Galuppi's*. It was deeply moving to see him in the remote place where he had passed his childhood as a boarder, 'always hungry and cold.' A place of burnings and freezings, the austere monochrome of the glorious resonant Lady Chapel was 'inspirational Maxine', especially when the troubled Michael Howard trained the choir. 'It was the icing on the cake', said James, 'even if we were mostly singing to the bats.'

Thanking me for his Ely bouquet and aware that I constantly travelled huge distances to see him in performance, he said with great satisfaction, 'You have come a very long way, Maxine, such a very long way to see me.'

When Arthur Wills retired in 1990 you returned for the occasion to sing *Here the Deities Approve* and Wills' *The Hound of Heaven*, with piano accompaniment, the Purcell having been your great 'opportunity' of initiation into the secular concert world at the age of sixteen. According to Arthur Wills you 'performed this with an outstanding flair and potency.'

Dr Wills had sent me a recording of his retirement concert when I had expressed interest in a commission from him. Many years later his 2007 memoir documented the *Galuppi* event: 'Another trip to hear a commission's first performance took Mary and I to Hinckley in Leicestershire where James Bowman was president of the Music Club. Here on the 24th September in Holy Trinity Church, he premiered *A Toccata of Galuppi's*. This was attended by Maxine Handy, who had commissioned the work in celebration of James' 50th birthday, with her family among the audience. James had requested a work with accompaniment for string quartet, and I acquiesced...'

Others have described your boyhood singing as 'characterful', even brilliant, but you have always modestly declared that you were 'nothing special'. When you went to New College to be interviewed for a choral scholarship they said to you, 'Why should we have you here when your academic record is so poor?' You answered, 'Please, will you hear me sing?' Thus you entered into the musical life of the Oxford Choirs and their crucial advantages. Christopher Campling, who left Ely to become Dean of Ripon Cathedral mentions you as a visiting artist there.

Ten years of exile in 'Crowned Ely' singing to the piano at choir practice, like the boys in Seamus Heaney's *The Bereaved*. The school a monastic, authoritarian environment – 'A terrible place of bullyings and beatings.'

In 1951 – Festival of Britain year, at the tender age of nine you lie awake in the dormitory listening to the other small boys crying for home.

Bravely you adjust and adapt – but never to the absence of *privacy*. Sent away as a vulnerable child, packed off without consent – leading to damaged adult patterns of withdrawal and loss of trust. Confined to the grim sanatorium with a throat infection, in mourning for the past. When, at last you came out your voice had broken.

'You have a boy, Maxine...a boy. You would never send your children away, because you would miss them too much...go mad without them', said James.

When I read Emily Dickinson's exquisite short poem *'Bind me I can still sing'* – it reminded me of James' courage, as an Ely chorister at 'the awkward age'. Emily's message is directed against oppression. Despite the violence and compulsion she endures, she manages to keep hold of her inner place, both physical and spiritual. Her voice and heart can never be removed, so she remains free:

> 'Bind me – I can still sing
> Banish – my mandolin strikes
>   true within
> Slay – and my
> Soul shall rise
> Chanting to Paradise –
> Still thine.'

You told me that when you went back to Ely it was 'like stepping into a dream'. You enjoyed retracing by car your old cross-country running route, remembering the sighting of the far Cathedral, a beacon of hope. This adult journey gave you immense satisfaction, now *you* were in control of the escape route. 'I remember one year when the river froze all the way from Ely to Cambridge', you said with yearning, thinking of your childhood. How you must have longed to skate all the way to King's College Chapel.

Telling me how much you loved the colour yellow and thanking me for the great joy of your Ely flowers, with their accompanying quotation from the *Book of Ruth*, you again made poignant reference to your boyhood:

'My mother never visited me, well hardly ever – because it was too far, Maxine, too far…'

Your disregard for dates is uncharacteristic of a history graduate but is part of your strange dislocated attitude to time, which arose perhaps from a longing for some lost and precious thing. This omission of fixed points makes you a biographers' nightmare, but you have always asserted that your biography is in your recordings. Those 'spotted with commonness' could be jealous and envious of your fame and pre-eminence, and they knew that like Shakespeare's *Coriolanus*, you were not at ease with the plebeian. '*I'm* always having to get rid of people' you said pointedly when seeing anyone with me of whom you disapproved. 'As I've told you many times, Maxine, you are a *pearl* amongst swine.'

James Bowman has never embraced populism or looked in the gutter for his repertoire. 'I would never do anything to bring the countertenor voice into disrepute', he has stated proudly. He has absolute contempt for the Philistine. Since being appointed a Gentleman of the Chapel Royal, in 2000, James has taken part in many great state occasions, including the annual service at the Cenotaph in Whitehall, where I glimpsed him in 2008. He has ignited the choir with whom he now sings regularly, and has recorded a superb disc of *Handel's Music for the Chapel Royal*. He is a joy to listen to, his splendour undiminished. Especially touching are his duets with the boy-treble voice, the sound of his own past. Several commissions by him for the choir and himself as soloist have included Giles Swayne's Christmas lullaby *O my dear heart*.

An earlier glimpse of James Bowman was from my living room sofa on 31st August 2007. He was taking part in the Service of Thanksgiving from the Guards' Chapel at London's Wellington Barracks, marking the Tenth Anniversary of the death of Diana, Princess of Wales. It was an odd occasion; a strange mix of private yet public ceremony. The service was broadcast live on BBC1 and ITV. I noted that James, in his beautiful red and white robes, was very much singing quietly, as part of the choir amidst flower arrangements that included living English garden roses, and rosemary for remembrance. But according to Bryan Appleyard in the September 2nd edition of *The Sunday Times*: 'Princes William and Harry apart, most people would rather not have been turning up to Diana's memorial service to bow once more to her popular power.'

20th September 1997 – The Marjorie King Memorial Concert

My gifts and cards for each special occasion contributed to a kind of tapestry or fresco, through which I developed complex patterns of interpretation, creating an intricate relationship with your work. 'I bring your cards to all my performances, Maxine. They are always so interesting'. And there they were inside your wonderful, battered, well-travelled music case. I almost expected to see written on the side, 'Please look after this countertenor'.

James had once warned me that Marjorie could be very rude, but luckily she 'approved' of me and was always most kind. Indeed, it was she who had formally introduced me to James in autumn 1992, twenty years after I had first heard him sing. Strangely, this was the same year that Robert King, then a twelve-year old boy treble, had first heard your voice when recording Purcell with you. This terrifying occasion had marked the commencement of his obsession and determination that one day, as adult keyboard player and conductor, he would work with you.

On the sad day of Marjorie's memorial concert to which James had invited me on 30 May 1997, saying 'I hope you will come, Maxine', I sent James yellow-in-blue flowers, accompanied by a beautiful card on which were written the words of Purcell's *Evening Hymn*. There had been a severe, nationwide shortage of flowers due to the recent death of Diana, Princess of Wales. During the concert interval you discussed with me the recent death from cancer of your friend and colleague, the lutenist Robert Spencer.

This had passed unnoticed outside musical circles and this deeply depressed James. 'They always mourn the wrong people, don't they Maxine' he said in melancholy tones. Robert had taught him more about the text than anybody, also to sit down for lute songs, to create a domestic duet. James missed him greatly.

As a special mark of his respect to me, James changed the programme to include Dowland's *Time stands still in gazing on her face* and concluded his recital with Purcell's *Evening Hymn*, just because I'd written it on his card. He told the audience that he had 'forgotten' his score for his intended encore, so would perform the *Evening Hymn* instead. His pretence was charming.

During the interval he had sat beside me and kissed his fingertips in a gesture of adoration for his flowers. 'They were the first thing to greet me this morning!' James emphasized his love of green as a musical colour, and asked me, 'Shall we mingle, Maxine?' Just as we were wondering whether or not to have a cup of tea, two female admirers of his seated behind us, attempted to speak to him. He rebuked them for their rude interruption, saying 'Do you mind! I'm speaking to my friend.' He then raised his score to screen us from their intrusive stare.

He continued to talk to me about his performance of Alan Ridout's *Soliloquy*, saying despondently, 'I am blue Maxine, that is what I am.' You were without your glasses and I'll always remember the remarkable lapis-blue of your eyes as they looked deeply into mine, with all the divine beauty of Leonardo's painting come to life. I wondered if they were your mother's eyes, handed down to you like ancestral jewels.

James' doleful mood informed our entire conversation and he expressed his anxiety that once he ceased to perform he would soon be forgotten. 'I've no idea how much longer I've got. *It* can go suddenly, like a boy's voice. Love for a voice is something very personal. It is a deeply personal thing. When I stop singing you won't want to know me, Maxine. I'll have to disappear and become a mystic memory.'

Also, he discussed with me his love of singing in Cathedrals. 'I love the very stones of Lincoln Cathedral and you Maxine are redolent with their spirituality', said James. His rare compliments were unforgettable.

Listening to his thoughts on Alan Ridout's *Soliloquy* I reflected on the vocal crisis that followed David Munrow's suicide at his home in Chesham Bois, on May 15th 1976. Much rumour and speculation surround his death, but the cause remains obscure. Robert King, who 'resuscitated' James Bowman's career in the 1980s, had an adolescent worship of David and his Early Music Consort. The 'pied piper' inspired his own love of period instruments and historically informed authentic performance. In his testimony, Robert King said 'James Bowman was the one in the know, but I never got out of James very much about Munrow. "David went mad", and that was it.' The Royal Academy of Music has an extensive archival collection of David Munrow's papers and letters, all accessible to the public. I'll look in on them when I'm next in London.

Grief and shock at the death of his dear friend led James to suffer a four year vocal crisis, which changed his voice forever. Some observers say that the sound by which Munrow had been obsessed was lost and gone, to be eventually replaced by something much more technically assured, darker, and with more colours. At the time, however, many thought that James Bowman's singing voice would never return. James describes his voice during this period as 'damaged to the point of destruction'. This can be clearly heard in his December 1977 recording of Handel's *Anthem for the Foundling Hospital*. His pivotal association with Britten and Munrow had lasted ten years. When they died in 1976 he was left in a deserted, but haunted place, like Henry James on Bellosguardo alone with his 'ghosts and glorious views', before he triumphantly re-emerged.

Certainly, James loved Geoffrey Burgon's very dark piece, *Merciless Beauty* because it combined the mediaeval and contemporary, but Munrow's specific mediaeval repertoire he never resurrected. The reasons for this avoidance were probably psychological as much as technical. Although James sometimes sounds indifferent and detached when confronted with others' problems, he actually has a remarkable and sensitive understanding of madness and disintegration. He felt for the desperation of Peter Pears after Britten's death.

'Good luck for your world premiere performance of Geoffrey Burgon's *Merciless Beauty*; I hope the Nightblue bouquet is beautiful and gives you pleasure,' I had taken immense trouble with the flower selection of 'only blue flowers' requested by James; he enjoyed setting me increasingly difficult tasks to give him pleasure. Though always immensely appreciative of my gifts to him he took pleasure in occasional warnings and gentle reprimands to assert his power over me.

During the interval he thanked me in private for my flowers and said that on his forthcoming birthday he would again like only two colours in austere juxtaposition, but this time 'blue and white'. He sat down beside me and affectionately touched my arm with his fingertips, telling me that he was worried about a numbness and tingling in his hand when he was holding his pen. He was anxious that it might be a forerunner of arthritis, from which his mother suffered. I reassured him that it was probably just repetitive-stress disorder. 'Too many years, James, of holding your score in freezing cathedrals', I said. I promised to consult my Doctor brother on his behalf. Knowing that my brother had a practice in his beloved Lake District, he said 'What a pity he isn't closer – I could travel to him for an examination and treatment.' As we contentedly leaned against each other he asked my permission to look inside my handbag. We played with the fantasy that one day he would come to my village and sing to me in one of the local churches. It was at this moment that I had my vision of him transformed into Leonardo's *Virgin of the Rocks*. I knew then that this ecstatic vision would probably never return, and was how I wished to remember him. I later described this to him in a letter: 'When I was sitting close to you a miraculous transformation took place, in which you changed into Leonardo's *Virgin of the Rocks*…the painting became a living thing and its watery wilderness moved.'

He explained to me his conviction that women understood and appreciated the countertenor voice much more than men because 'with women there isn't the problem of masculinity.' Indeed, women have been his major celebrants. The synaesthetic Jane Mackay has interpreted his *Dream* arias with two watercolour paintings, and the portrait artist June Mendoza has depicted him seated in front of one of his model theatres, holding a miniature of his Glyndebourne *Oberon*, like a talisman. In my case, he praised and admired my 'impeccable taste', 'exquisite manners' and 'perfection in language', also telling me of his further aspirations. James identifies with women but he has a horror of female domination.

20th October 1997

I posted a D H Lawrence poem by which he was fascinated, also promising to search for his birthday white and blue. The male florist who personally arranged the flowers and delivered to James commented admiringly on my sublime combination of bouquet and quotation:

'Like a flame blown whiter and whiter
In a deeper and deeper darkness.
Evermore exquisite, distilled in separation,'

His love of chiaroscuro was memorably evoked when, on Radio 3, he discussed his live performance of Elizabeth Lutyens' *The Tears of Night*. 'I like the sort of *chiaroscuro* feeling, of one moving from darkness into light all the time through a sort of twilight'. My need for closeness followed by aloneness mirrored that of James. He complained that by 'living in the wilds of Cheshire' rather than near him in the South-East I limited our contact. 'You come to me, Maxine, not I to you. *I* am the great artist', he said with mock-imperiousness, as he stood beside a stone pillar in Grantham church. James was well aware that he baffled and he beckoned, knowing that I would always answer his irresistible call. He further tantalised me with suggestions that closer proximity might enable us to meet up for the theatre, or see an opera together, such as the forthcoming *Turn of the Screw*. 'We are brief encounter, Maxine, that is what we are', he concluded in tones of childlike disappointment.

To sustain a friendship with James it was necessary to intrigue him and win his trust; like his own description of singing Bach, he is 'full of pitfalls for the unwary.' During a telephone conversation he told me that he was packing, as he was shortly departing for Belgium: 'a horrible place, the only thing they're good at is making chocolates. Do you like chocolates, Maxine? I'll bring some back for you.' No matter how often James switched from verbal embrace to denial I'd place these memories in a special chamber and make them beautiful. 'I'm loved and adored. Thank you for your kindness and devotion to me, Maxine. I'll endeavour to deserve it. I don't care about the world, not while I still have you. Write to me always and never stop adoring me. I find you wonderfully remote from all other people'.

In performance, when I was part of the audience he said that he wanted us to be 'as close to each other as possible.' Such was his emphasis on intimate communion with his listener. Once at Bolton on October 11th 1992 he abruptly moved sideways in order to be directly in front of me, whilst singing his encore, Bach's *Erbarme dich*. To avoid a collision with James, the violinist had to quickly slide backwards in his chair. James thought that when I was not attending his concerts, I should be at home writing and listening to his recorded work. He confided that I was the only person in England who sent him flowers. 'Someone loves and adores you, Mr Bowman', said his local florist after delivering yet another exquisite arrangement, this time with 'a touch of red' for Christmas.

For many of his bouquets I used quotations and themes from his arias. His favourite amongst Handel's English oratorios was *Theodora*. So on two occasions the flowers were adorned with an aria and love duet for his character Didimus, but addressing him as Theodora, myself assuming the role of Didimus. James enjoyed the gender reversal of so many of my offerings; he thought it 'delightfully Handelian.'

In response to beautiful yellow roses for Handel's *Joseph and his Brethren*, sent with a favourite card of the ancient Egyptian 'opening of the mouth ceremony', which appealed to James' twin preoccupation with singing and eating, he gave me three wonderful 'singing photographs' of himself at work – with wide opened mouth – At the Paris Opera in concert performance with Jean-Claude Malgoire's La Grande Ecurie et la Chambre du Roy. In Handel's *Ariodante* at Geneva, and as *Oberon* in a famous production at Covent Garden. In all three photos chiaroscuro is effected with the use of Rembrandt lighting:

To James –
   Your beautiful portrait at the Paris Opera…is gloriously laurelled in black and dove. *Ariodante* is similarly honoured in black and cloud.
   - Oberon dazzles!!

   You made the role of *Oberon* your own. Peter Hall described your magic wood as 'a dangerous place of strange alterations.' The Purcellian aria 'I know a bank' is central to your identification with the Fairy King. It is a lyrical evocation of this beautiful place in the forest, in order to create a horrible transformation and humiliate Tytania. The music critic and writer Norman Lebrecht warns us 'Never let yourself be overwhelmed by beauty, or some artist will use it to destroy you.' Oberon's 'love-juice' always put me in mind of Henry James' dream/nightmare in the Napoleonic Galerie d'Apollon in the Louvre, his true home. Anyway, it inspired many of my summer-solstice flowers:

Dear Maxine
   Thank you for the lovely Roses - a memory of 'Midsummer Nights'.
   They are just beginning to open to me.
   James

   You inscribed my CD booklet of your long awaited recording 'in remembrance of past enchantments'.

The Library
   I gave him many inscribed books to celebrate his *Dream*. 'You have opened my eyes to books' he told me, 'and above all I love the beauty of what you give me.'

This wide-ranging library included enchanting children's literature, Primo Levi, Elie Wiesel and everything by and about Henry James:

'Thank you for the latest Henry James Biography. I am now rapidly acquiring a comprehensive Henry James Library. I shall call it the Maxine Handy Library. I will take it to Paris with me when I go for the Dream.'

I decided not to see James in performance in France. I dislike noisy French audiences and preferred his Englishness to remain in his own country. He has always said that much as he loves working and travelling in France he could never live anywhere but England. He told me that he was grateful to the French for in effect 'paying me for what I do in my own country' but regards French as an awkward sung language. For his 25th Anniversary concert at St John's he chose a baroque repertoire of Purcell, Handel, and Bach – a much more intellectual programme than for the French occasion.

I imagined him singing in France, dazzled by the bejewelled audience in over-ornamented venues like the Paris Opera. Or in Italy – looking at the most beautiful view in the world and perhaps listening to the bells of Florence saying 'Gloriani, Gloriani' in homage. Then the world-renowned artist – the living legend returns home to the South-East where my flowers await him in his porch, on the threshold to welcome him home.

Through his green front door. In his private domain the two large-eared Abyssinian Cats are waiting, always seeming to listen as you are practising at your piano. I imagine you singing *Sweeter than Roses*. Knowing of your enthusiasm for model theatres – I gave you my treasured collection of programmes from the time of Laurence Olivier's directorship of the Old Vic. You were deeply touched by this gift.

February 1993

Bach's *St Matthew Passion* in Jonathan Miller's dramatisation in-the-round, at once became a rare setting for James' alto solo 'Erbarme dich', supported by a glorious string accompaniment. He promised that for the entire first-night performance he would sing to me, adding that as there were three more performances to come he could certainly 'skip one in-the-round'.

It was just before his first performance in Holy Trinity Church, Chelsea, in February 1993, that James spoke the words which conveyed our remarkable empathy as artist and audience. As I entered the church he called my name and gestured to me to come to him:

'Maxine! Show me where you're sitting and I'll open my mouth very wide and sing to you...My live performances should leave you in suspended ecstasy, waiting for the next time...They live and then die like a flower, but there should never be any sense of anti-climax'.

His beautiful words still resonate within me. I have written them down and keep them always in my handbag, in memory of a *cosa mentale*. For me they relate directly to the painting which expressed the way in which I uniquely *saw* him, and also the way in which he looked at me:

'You see what I am, Maxine. I do my work for people like you who truly appreciate what I do. Seen through your eyes, Maxine, I *am* Leonardo's beautiful *Virgin of the Rocks*, and yes I agree with you entirely but it sounds much lovelier coming from you.' In Easter 1997 James gave me a copy of *The James Bowman Collection*. It included his recording of Bach's 'Erbarme dich', of which I had been unaware. It was a complete and thrilling Easter surprise.

Ripon Cathedral March 2nd 1991

He had sent me this engagement by post, and it turned out to be a life changing experience. We had spoken on the phone several times and I had sent flowers to his home, but we had yet to meet.

On a rainy and sleeting Saturday, freezing in the Cathedral, I attended the afternoon rehearsal – or preparation – would be a more accurate term. When my friends and I entered the cold Cathedral I observed him at once.

Godlike and immensely tall, wearing a long green gabardine coat and tartan scarf, but with touchingly childlike red shoelaces on his large feet. He was singing the Amen sequence from Vivaldi's *Stabat Mater*, followed by the remarkable *mouse* solo from Britten's *Rejoice in the Lamb*. My request for the following day, to hear him on Radio 3 in Britten's canticle *Abraham and Isaac*, from the original 1972 National Gallery recital 'Songs for three Voices', had been successful. I was informed by the Master of the Choristers that he knew of the Sunday broadcast, and was highly pleased. I was unaware at this time that James Bowman thought of this 1972 recital as one of the musical highlights of his entire career.

Every year I asked Radio 3 to play something by you, at Midsummer and on your birthday; they always complied. On October 27th 1993 Ted Perry of Hyperion Records wrote to me. 'I salute your enterprise and championship of James. That's devotion and I respect that.' Robert King, from whom I received a number of enthusiastic letters, described James as 'the voice of the Purcell series, whether in ensemble or singing solo.' All these years later his impact is just as extraordinary; his eternal splendour has ignited the Choir of the Chapel Royal.

After almost two years of correspondence, flowers, occasional telephone conversations, speculative glances and exchanges, we were at last introduced at Hinckley on Saturday 19th September 1992. It was a delightful event; an intimate lute recital with Robert Spencer, that 'most poetic and subtle of lutenists'.

In 1993 I travelled to Brentwood Catholic Cathedral in Essex, just to hear him sing Scarlatti's *Salve Regina*. In the same year I went all the way to Snape Maltings and back again in one day, just to hear the Scarlatti piece, which he subsequently recorded on Hyperion.

His late forties and fifties were a golden time, especially for his recordings of Handel, such as 'Heroic Arias', 'English Arias', and 'Italian Duets', all recorded on the Hyperion label. In conversation with me in the crypt of St John's, Ted Perry said that only James Bowman could perform Handel's 'Italian Duets' because they were so impossibly difficult. Ted added that in his opinion they were James' greatest recording. Eva Schay Mayer, my friend, and for many years a violinist with the ENO, told me recently that she is indifferent to the sound of the countertenor voice, 'except that of James Bowman.'

Sunday 7th March 1993

Late one afternoon at the small church of St Giles, Cripplegate, you performed Britten's *Abraham and Isaac*. An amusing incident had occurred just before the beginning of the concert. A very large harp was needed for Britten's canticle *The Death of Narcissus*, to be performed later on. This harp, already in place was obscuring our view of each other, despite my front-row seat. So, having taken the platform in black tie and tails ready to sing to me, you smilingly lifted up the harp and moved it far away from our line of vision. Afterwards, you came over to talk and kneel beside me, gazing at my Siamese cat brooch. You ignored my friend's attempt to address some remarks to you, scornfully cutting him dead before giving me a fond farewell.

Again in 2003 – on Monday November 8th at King's College Chapel, Cambridge, James entered down the Nave and as he passed by me, bent down to whisper '"The Agnus Dei" is for you, Maxine'. Together we would enter the inner sanctum. During the interval he come over to thank me for his birthday flowers, and say that he had sent me 'a very special card'. Seating himself beside me he raised his score to shield us from an adjacent couple in the audience whom he described angrily as 'trying to intrude on us.' As he withdrew for the second half he gave my travelling companion a hostile and dismissive glare, later saying to me on the telephone: 'I *saw* him, trying to lean against you...I felt like hitting him...hitting him.' James can be very aggressive, bear grudges, and have a hot-temper, but his protectiveness towards me was deeply touching and wholly reciprocated, especially as he had survived Ely – the 'Dark Land' in Geoffrey Hill's *Canaan* collection. I was devoted to James as I was to my beloved children.

Some few weeks ago in April 2009 I watched a fascinating documentary on the strange relationship between Baroness Pannonica de Koenigswarter (nee Rothschild) and the genius jazz musician Thelonious Monk. She was a mysterious figure; her entomologist father chose to name her after a fragile moth with yellow wings. 'Nica' was deeply unconventional and 'the moth' turned out to be an apt metaphor for a woman who was in love with the night and adored cats. Thelonious Monk suffered from an erratic mental condition now known as bipolar disorder. Because he was manic-depressive he imposed huge demands on those who came into close contact with him. Nica had become obsessed with Monk's composition *Round Midnight*; it took her two years to meet him after she first heard the recording in 1952. Thenceforth, Nica became his unstinting ally and devotee. Her life changed forever.

Pannonica's niece, Hannah Rothschild, the maker of this very moving documentary, is to tell this story again in a book to be published in 2010. Her great aunt, who was married and the mother of five children before she encountered Monk, was deliberately forgotten in the Rothschild archives. Thelonious Monk was also already married with two children when he met Nica, and Hannah believes that their contact was entirely platonic: 'My feeling' Hannah says, 'is that when she heard *Round Midnight* she had the musical equivalent of an epiphany – this sound unlocked feelings. It said, "I understand your anger, your feelings of isolation, your sadness." If you look at the photographs she looks at him adoringly...there's no doubt in my mind that she loved him...But sex doesn't always have to come into it.' I look forward to reading Hannah's book; it has taken her ten years of research to overcome the silence which surrounds this unlikely and intriguing friendship.

An uncomfortable dark silence had always existed within Monk's mind and his eccentricities verged on insanity. Mental illness had created the original connection between Pannonica and Thelonious. They were drawn together by problems until their souls enjoyed a Donne-like mingling. Nica shared her apartment with over 306 cats, whilst worshipping Monk's music with religious intensity. He wrote and dedicated a piece for her titled *Pannonica*. Thelonious spent the final seven years of his life until his death in 1982, in near total silence – not speaking or playing a note to anyone. During this prolonged torment, some of it spent in hospital, Pannonica saw little of him, but wept ceaselessly as though he had already died. She still had his recorded music and beautiful memories, but he himself was largely lost to her. Before her own death in 1988 she left instructions that her ashes must be scattered 'Around Midnight.'

James Bowman is extremely sensitive about the way he is 'looked at'. To some people the male high voice is not sublime, but ridiculous. Even he, the greatest countertenor of all time, with a sound unlike and unmatched by any other, is 'terrified of being laughed at.' I had seen this happen only rarely, and usually in some unappealing small-town venue, such as Ilkley on Wednesday February 11th 1998 in the King's Hall. Unresponsive provincial Yorkshire found falsetto absurd and very weird. They probably thought that the King's Consort singer was a eunuch. James had warned me that it would be 'a ghastly occasion with ghastly people.' After the recital he invited me to walk outside with him. He smiled, taking my arm affectionately, then just as suddenly moved away, saying 'You bring me into conflict with myself', a remark I have never understood. Within James there existed a paradoxical combination of vulnerability with superiority in his relations with others. He is remarkably modest and endearingly unpretentious. A man of true humility and wonderful humour, never interested in 'the trappings of success'. But a combination of two opposing impulses – 'Stay with me' and 'Keep your distance' resulted in a turbulent mixture of defensive narcissism and a desperate need to break out of painful isolation.

'All that I have written is as nothing to you' I said, deeply hurt. He denied this. 'Don't be ridiculous, did I ever say that', he replied with sweet emphasis. 'We have something very beautiful, Maxine. Why let other people spoil it?'

However, he conceded that I was right about the atmosphere at Ilkley and expressed remorse for his anger towards me, adding 'Are you saying that I'm defiling myself by appearing in such venues? Why do you tell me such things? I brood on them for months. I *know* what they are thinking when they look at me – what an odd looking man with a peculiar voice. I expect you to protect me Maxine.'

The whole scene between us outside in the moonlight resembled Britten's *Dream,* in which Oberon torments Tytania for her perceived injury. 'Jealous Oberon' having secured the disputed 'lovely boy' and regained control, begins to pity Tytania's infatuation and awakens her from her dream. They celebrate their restored friendship with a dance in the sylvan World of Shadows.

'Sound, music. Come, my queen, take hands with me
And rock the ground where on these sleepers be.
Now thou and I are new in amity.'

I quoted these words of Oberon back at him, myself assuming the role of the Fairy King, and addressing him as 'Tytania'. This brought a momentary delightful smile to his face, and we shook hands. 'Our conflict is resolved, Maxine. Come to my *Dream*, and to the *Blake Songs* at Snape on Easter Monday…' But as we said goodnight and he accused himself of having so unfairly misunderstood me, I told him that he had made me cry. 'Good' he said, 'you deserve it, you deserve to suffer. You are too emotional, like David Munrow.' He then embraced me with some surprising last words. 'Write to me always and never stop adoring me.'

The mystical union between James and myself resembled a relationship from the Middle Ages. At his Burgon recital at High Wycombe, which had opened with lines from Chaucer, he gave me a large card of Gloucester Cathedral's East Window. His idea of paradise was to sit beneath this window, which commemorated the fallen at Crécy, and listen to Vaughan Williams' *Fantasia on a theme by Thomas Tallis*. He inscribed my card:

'For Maxine
　　The essence of Mediaevel inspiration and ecstasy'
　　James

He sent me Christmas cards depicting the infant Jesus being read to by his mother, or blissfully asleep in her arms, and once told me that I was Mary and he was Jesus. In any event we had the correct initials! He exalted and idealised me, which was charming.

Certainly, James tender singing of a lullaby, cradle song, or Hymn to the Virgin is unsurpassable, whether it be by Burgon, Bach, Byrd, or Anon, as it is on the plangent, recent disc *Songs for Ariel* (2005). When I listen to his profound interpretation of the *Hymn to Mary*, I imagine him in the Lady Chapel at Ely, 'singing to the bats.' James sings with his whole body, often seeming to achieve a trance like state; it is a glorious thing and I'll always remember it.

Only two weeks ago I came across a deeply moving poem by Ahmad Waheed, written at the Ted Hughes Arvon Centre in Heptonstall, West Yorkshire. It was part of *Metamorphosis*, an anthology of new writing funded by the Medical Foundation for the Care of Victims of Torture. I thought that it would be a marvellous piece for James, if set by Geoffrey Burgon or Giles Swayne.

Words of Lullaby
  I remember the time
  When you were breaking the distances
  By your innocent smiles
  Slowly, slowly approaching me.

  I love the time
  When I was covering you
  With the words of lullaby
  Till your eyes were saying goodbye
  To the world of life.

On so many thrilling occasions you stood right in front of my first row seat to give me the pearls of your repertoire, opening up the intimate space of your mouth, wider and still wider, 'an unnatural sound perfected until it sounds natural.' I felt grateful to the renowned and complex Michael Howard, for five years your choirmaster at Ely. He had given you a thorough grounding in technique, always paying attention to dramatic interpretation and diction. 'Lips, Tongue and Teeth' was his distinctive *aide memoir*.

Despite his many friends and huge musical circle, an aura of loneliness surrounded James, probably essential to his creativity. 'He is definitely more moon than sun' my mother observed. Many of his cards to me expressed this, as had his May 1987 recording of Purcell's solo setting of the visionary text by Kathryn Philips, *O Solitude*. When I used it to accompany his flowers, he told me that he adored the words of this poem and that they reminded him of 'us'. He used to tease me about my complete lack of sense of direction, and going everywhere by taxi in London because I never understood distance and location. In contrast, he was very practical, loved his car, and could mentally map the details of any route. When I became confused by topography, he said with humour and kindness, 'Well, Maxine, if you are a mystic I suppose it doesn't matter where you are!'

I'll always treasure the memory of his 50th birthday recital at the Old Royal Naval College Chapel on Tuesday November 12th 1991. Trevor Pinnock and the English Concert were his accompanists. Trevor Pinnock said that James would want to say a few words to the audience on this special occasion; in fact he said nothing! Before the recital I had seen James in his elegant long green gabardine, walking quickly towards the railway station in the torrential evening rain. Obviously, Trevor Pinnock and his musicians had not turned up, and James was in search of them.

For his Handel and Purcell concert on August 3rd 1994, at the Royal Hall in Harrogate, I had sent flowers and a card saying: 'I hope the flowers give you pleasure – roses to remind you of your ravishing interpretations of Purcell's music.' As I approached the evening's venue I glimpsed him walking gloomily toward the artists' entrance. Seen from behind, without his singer's hyper-expressive face he seemed shrouded in melancholy. My mother said 'He looks as though he is going to his own hanging.' When he saw me in the auditorium he gave me a wonderful smile of welcome. Joy and gratitude shone from him. Afterwards, he'd run after me but I'd already left. 'I saw you in the Hall looking ecstatic. I ran after you but you'd already gone', he told me later.

During the interval of the *Marjorie King Memorial Concert*, James had asked me what I had in my carrier bag. When I handed him a copy of *Benjamin Britten's Poets – the poetry he set to music*, he asked to write an inscription for me. James said that he wanted to think carefully 'in private' so he took my book to the vestry at the rear of the church, and during a break in his performance he inscribed it for me. 'To Maxine – withdrawn for a season, but always attentive and receptive. 20/9/97. He said that he wanted it to be ambiguous. 'It might apply to either of us...We have both had serious problems and suffered withdrawal after a terrible loss.'

David Munrow's handbells made their appearance at this concert. 'It seems a long time ago now, Maxine, such a long time ago since David died. I'm always thinking of him.' I asked James about the Gordon Crosse Memorial piece which he had first performed at Hinckley on 24th January 1985; I have a recording of it from BBC archives. Crosse's heartfelt songs were inspired and influenced by the instruments of David Munrow's Early Music Consort. The piece is very much a personal response to David's death; the anguished and ghostly recorder playing accompanies James' voice until it slowly darkens and fades, and the recorder is alone. 'It's very austere music', James said. 'I remember the bells being quite haunting at the end. He was clever, Gordon, in the way he summoned up the spirit of David in a rather melancholy way.' The man closest to my heart has gone mad.

You then touched briefly on the unhappy thought of retirement, wincing as you mentioned the word. I reminded him that neither Alfred Deller nor our mutual idol Peter Pears had retired; they had continued in performance until accepted by Persephone's dark chamber. 'And your gift James', I said, 'seems immortal.' Shaking his head, and with his lower lip protruding, he replied gravely: 'One day I will have to disappear and become a mystic memory – but not yet. I've no idea how much longer I've got. It can go quite suddenly like a boy's voice. When I cease to sing you won't want to know me, Maxine.'

I was concerned by his mood of despondency; he said that I was the colour of sunlight and he was the lovely blue. 'Blue – that is what I am, Maxine...' he repeated. 'Unlike almost all people, Maxine, you have never sought to take advantage of me...unfortunately for me most of my friends are neurotics.' Brightening suddenly like the sun shining through glass, he became a mediaeval metaphor for Christ within the Virgin, saying, 'Yes Maxine we must renounce things. Jamesian renunciation, we believe in it!'

James was well aware that he was thought by some to be an arrogant and 'careless user', who ignored or overlooked those people to whom he should have shown lifetime gratitude. In my case he tried hard to be an 'attentive soul'. At this time he regarded me as a precious, trusted listener, and was keen to respond to and share my literary enthusiasm. 'I read everything you send me' he said, 'and I'm becoming very fond of dear old Henry James. I promise to read all his letters...I'm gradually working through them one by one.' On other occasions, however, he complained of being 'inundated' and overwhelmed. 'It's all becoming a bit much' he complained, admitting to being 'a slow reader'. Arthur Wills said with great amusement, 'I'm amazed he's reading at all, Maxine, he certainly wasn't at Ely!'

Most importantly, James let me know that he shared my epiphanies; they were not mine alone. When things were perfect James too ascended to a seemingly unattainable realm – our Jamesian apotheosis. 'When things are perfect, Maxine, it is for me just as it is for you, as you describe it', he said.

In the concluding lines of Geoffrey Burgon's Dramatic Scena for Countertenor *Nearing the Upper Air* (1988) James' emphasis on the drawn out word 'f-l-e-d' imitates the sounds of a fading male orgasm and withdrawal, as the soul of Orpheus leaves his body. 'Maxine, what is your favourite sensation in the whole world?' James once asked. 'Orgasm', I replied. 'Quite so', he said. 'Mine too.' James once described Nirvana as 'a never-ending spiritual orgasm.' He was always able to combine the physical with the spiritual, using his whole body to sing and working on every syllable. My recording of Burgon's Scena, which uses Virgil's version of the Orpheus and Eurydice legend, is inscribed: 'For Maxine, "That Voice cried out." James'.

My singer told me that of all the things I'd written and said to him, there was one that he loved above all others and would never forget: 'When I come to your live performances, James, only you look alive. All around you seems dead and vanishes from my sight.' He responded to these words by sending me a card of a solitary golden-leafed birch tree, everything around it dark and lifeless. It was his delightful way of acknowledging that he understood how I loved him, that I felt surrounded by his light. Neither he nor I *ever* expressed any interest in the 'sexuality' of the countertenor voice. We did not think about it. James told me that it was another thing that made us alike: 'For this is not one life; nor do I always know if I am man or woman...so strange is the contact of one with another.' (Rilke) However, although the gender of his alto voice is irrelevant, James *always* sounds like a man. Everything about him is hyper-masculine.

He admitted his resemblance to Oberon in his sadism and occasional spitefulness. Having inflicted damage on others he simply withdraws, and disappears without explanation. 'You have great charm, Maxine, and I have none' he once told me, quickly adding, 'You are highly intelligent and frighteningly perceptive...I wouldn't want you to think I'm clever...I only got into Oxford because of my voice.' His candour was touching, especially when he admitted 'I can't imagine why anybody would want to visit me at home...' It is my belief that only self-censorship prevented James from voicing Sviatoslav Richter's verdict 'I do not like myself.'

James has said 'I often sound insane when I'm singing' and the idea that intermittently he was slightly mad increased my protective feeling towards him; it is a terrible thing to be lonely and unprotected. 'I expect your devotion and support, Maxine' he said. 'I need to be protected by you.'

The *dark-light* tone should always be present in the singing voice; it was certainly there in our contact. The warmth of my living, breathing, responsiveness to himself, he valued highly, but in 'the chill of his egotism and the light of her use.' Beneath the cold winter moonlight in Ilkley, with your hand gently clasping my arm, you had said in a passionate outburst: 'My work is the most important thing in my life, Maxine; it comes before everything. I cannot return others feelings for me.'

James has always resisted any suggestion of a conventional biography, saying that it doesn't interest him. 'I don't want people fingering my private life,' he said to me. James proudly asserts that his biography is in the huge number of recordings he's made. On his very recent CD *Songs for Ariel* each track has a passionate personal meaning, a 'host of pictures from his life and career.' It includes Purcell's *Sweeter than Roses* and *Here the Deities Approve*.

My decade of letters to him, locked away in a large box, in the privacy of his study, documents a unique period of exalted receptivity during which not a detail was lost: 'a feeling so intense, in letter after letter, that it verged on a sort of ecstasy, strange and extraordinarily sustained.' James described me over this decade as 'tracing each herb and flower', using his own words from an aria recorded on Handel's *English Arias*.

'I keep all your correspondence Maxine, including the envelopes. It is very beautiful and always so interesting. One day, when I've finished with *all this* I'm going to edit and compile a book from your letters, to be left after my lifetime.' James used the phrase *all this* to refer both to his work and my written response to it.

During one of his depressive phases I sent James a multicoloured bouquet, accompanied by the following words from Milton's *Comus* 1634:

For James and Handel

'That in the colours of the rainbow live
And play i' th' plighted clouds'

James adored my Miltonic quote which so perfectly described his symbiotic relationship with Handel. Theirs was a musical love affair made in heaven. He responded with a glorious card depicting a rainbow above the stormy Ardamurchan peninsula. Sometimes he said to me 'You and I are playing.'

My favourite Handelian roles for James were those written for the famous contralto castrato, Senesino. James said that when singing a role written for Senesino, he could work out the original sound from reading and studying the score. 'I can hear Senesino's voice in the music, such as in the title role of Handel's *Guilio Cesare* and *Orlando*.'

I never worshipped James more completely than in his performance of the disturbed and childlike *Orlando*, described by him as 'like being inside a melancholy cocoon – I love that.' In Act Three comes the hauntingly memorable 'Già l'ebro mio ciglio', sung by Orlando. In the anguish of unrequited love he furiously throws the compassionate Angelica into a gloomy cave, and determines on suicide. As he descends into madness, the direct effect of his jealous obsession, he is given repose under the influence of a narcotic and sleeps on a stone:

Già l'ebro mio ciglio
Quel dolce liquore
Invita a posar

My booklet of the recording is 'suitably inscribed' by James:

'For Maxine
In her Cave'

James' falsetto is perfect for so many of the full-blooded heroic castrato roles in Baroque Opera. Physically static, all the drama comes from within the voice in a series of *da capo* arias which explore and develop character and motivation. The repetition with minimum ornamentation, and James' dislike of 'over-ornamentation of any kind', combine to rise to a thrilling climax. Even the great Janet Baker as *Guilio Cesare* lacks the eroticism of the male high voice. Whilst reclaiming Baroque repertoire from basses, tenors, and women, James has also developed the solo possibilities of the countertenor in 20th-21st century music.

A beautiful and personal thing

'Come to my *Dream*, Maxine, and *The Blake Songs* at Snape on Easter Monday. Do you have your ticket for the *Dream*? I'll get you one and send it to you…'

Over the telephone, as James gave me a definitive list of his 1998 engagements, which included the 'Awake Sweet Love' recital at Snape Maltings on Easter Monday, 13th April 1998, he said: 'My face is all covered in shaving foam, Maxine', and told me that in the privacy of his own home he often talked to himself, whistled and hummed. I remember his speaking voice suddenly changed from baritone to head voice as though Oberon had taken over on the phone! A rare loss of vocal control, which was somehow thrilling. James went on to say how immensely important to him the Britten connection was, and how it had been the foundation of our empathy. The 1972 National Gallery recital of *Sweeter than Roses* and

Abraham and Isaac, a perfect mixture of the mortal and divine, with Peter Pears, was the mutual musical highlight of our lives. Charmingly, James said 'Your love for my voice is a beautiful and personal thing, like the 1972 recital which inspired it.'

I gave James a wonderful 1976 postcard of Britten in a wheelchair, holding a posy of pink roses. 'That's just how I remember him', he said, and promised to treasure it all his life. He also promised that he would never forget my childhood story about the solace of falling snow. 'I promise to remember that always Maxine, did it help?' He told me that his mother was dying…'My mother's funeral is arranged down to the last detail – her coffin is to be completely covered in snowdrops,' the flowers symbolic of re-birth and consolation. In James Joyce's short story *The Dead*, Gabriel stands at the window to watch the falling snow, and meditates on the relationship of death and love. The snow, which he watches mesmerically falling and dissolving, provides an image of resolution. On the Feast of Epiphany, January 6th 1904, in Dublin, Gabriel accepts his transience as snow falls 'on all the living and the dead.'

Easter Monday

I arose at dawn on Easter Monday, as the recital was to begin at 11.30 am. James looked for me in the audience and having immediately found me, he had sung to me as he promised. Afterwards, I saw him sitting at a table in the sunlit foyer, his head resembling the Farnese Antinous. I had sent him yellow in blue to celebrate my favourite 20th century song cycle, the recording of which was very much his own project and dear to his heart. He rebuked me for not attending his recent concert *Dream*, for which he had offered to send me a ticket. 'You didn't come to my Dream. I missed you there. It was a magical occasion, but of course you didn't come.'

Sitting alone in his white gabardine and wearing glasses he looked unbearably solitary and morose, despite signing concert programmes for his queuing, waiting public. I said goodbye and turned to go when he suddenly called me back, saying, 'Maxine, give me a kiss before you go.' I embraced him with a kiss and held him in my arms, tenderly pressing my face against his cheek. This was our farewell; he was as cold and unresponsive as stone.

Wrapping my soft, burgundy scarf around me, as he had wrapped me in the dignity of his art, I stepped outside into the solace of gently falling snow. Like Henry James, so long ago, I walked briefly on forlorn Dunwich beach. A childhood memory of my mother also returned to me, and a description of the incident that I'd written for my singer in response to hearing him perform Geoffrey Burgon's *Almost Peace*. He had told me that he loved its mystical beauty and in mythologizing my mother it expressed our further empathy. Whenever I heard James sing the Burgon setting of Emily Dickinson's poems, it reconnected me with those intensities and the brief-encounters I had enjoyed with James. Together, in imagination, we had revisited fragments form the classical world and childhood, travelling through time, elegizing friends.

'Let the Moths flutter round your gabardine – until like snowflakes they form a silent storm around the light.'

Peter Ackroyd, *Hawksmoor*

Saturday 27th February 1999

Ten years ago in the King's Hall of the Armstrong Building at Newcastle University. Close to leafy Jesmond where you spent your formative years enrolled at four years of age in the choir of St Nicholas Cathedral. I suspect that Newcastle has a malevolence inherited from James' childhood in constant exile, 'an unpleasant or unhappy atmosphere may persist like some noisome scent in the air...'

Sent away to Ely.

Always singing in the summer holidays – 'Hasn't your voice broken yet?' said your mother.

In February 1999

You were David in Handel's *Saul* –

Healing the wounded soul of the king with your singing and playing.

'To wound a soul is as great a criminal act as killing a body', said a Jewish survivor of Auschwitz.

Formalities preserved us 'Hello, Maxine, thank you for coming,' he said – but did not sing to me.

I departed through the revolving door, and watched him go, encircled by a coterie, turning his back on me like a dark-faced god, echoing Edna O'Brien's *The girl with the green eyes*. It was a tenebrous cessation of contact 'leaving me alone like a man new fallen from fairyland in the black darkness of night.'

During Tenebrae in Holy Week fifteen candles, fitted on a triangular frame, are extinguished one by one until the service ends in darkness. James had sometimes presided at this ritual in his local church, St Mary's. By the end of 2000 I was alone in the dark holy triangle. In the words of Geoffrey Hill, the great English poet, and my former Shakespeare tutor: 'Overnight the inmost self made outcast,'

All the reading, all the dreaming had been in preparation for your arrival. How wonderful that he looks at me and sings to me. I felt your attention surround me even when you were absent. I felt myself to be a part of your quest...your creation. How could you disappear, cease to sing to me? I had known the focus of your mind and understood its complex symbolism. Your treatment of each syllable a revelation.

The Story of a Masterpiece

In 1998, in a letter to the great singer, I alluded to *The Story of a Masterpiece*, by Henry James. I had given him an inscribed copy of the novella which takes the idea of an Old Master portrait, suspended there and slowly fading. I wrote to him saying, 'It's so perfectly true, that as you slowly fade and your voice darkens with age like the tones of an "old master", you become an ever more beautiful Masterpiece,'

Listening to Radio 3 'Artist in Focus: James Bowman', the countertenor likened himself in April 2002 to an old painting fading: 'I think all voices sink and all voices get colours over the years. It's like an old painting fading. I feel like an old Masterpiece hanging there...' Either consciously or unconsciously, in his BBC interview with Brian Kay in 2002, James had used the idea in my 1998 letter to him, of his resemblance to an 'Old Master'. James Bowman's shrine is my print of Leonardo's *The Virgin of the Rocks*, framed deep inside an arch of holly green and reeded dark wood. This precious and adored painting, which hangs on an upstairs wall, has replaced the many photographs of James, which he had given to me.

The end of a decade came – in a precisely dated green letter – 6th October 1999.

As overwhelming as the memory itself has remained of poetic precision...

A cruel reminder of memory – but not mystic.

My desolate thoughts returned to Greenwich and seeing his green gabardine disappearing into the November night.

The colour of life, hope, and renewal mingling in the rain symbolising loss.

I remembered that after his performance of my commission to celebrate his 50th birthday, he had invited me to join him in a bow, wrapping me for a moment in the glittering mantle of his fame. Oscar Wilde had said 'It is through Art, and through Art only, that we can realize our perfection.'

Music made a beautiful and personal thing
 - as it was in my letters to him
 - and his singing to me –

The Library at Night

I used to imagine him seated at his desk reading my letters, resembling the painting *Portrait of a Gentleman in his Study*, by Lorenzo Lotto, from the Galleria dell' Accademia, Venice. This exquisite gallery, a favourite of Henry James, contains a number of paintings by Giorgione, an enigmatic artist beloved of Sir Peter Pears and James Bowman; his palette of luminous blues a voyage somewhere else.

I wondered if James had ever imagined me at home, pen in hand, bent over my writing whilst listening to his recorded work. I like to think that *Burning in Blueness – The Dark-Light of a Countertenor*, from which these brief-encounters are derived, is my 'fine-art' memorial to James: for his eyes only.

In the absence of his music and the melancholy of a dream – I entered my singer's house to be reunited with *The Maxine Handy Library* and ten years of handwritten letters. All was bathed in terracotta light, evoking the ruined tombs along the Via Appia Antica, and the vanished Semitic Civilisation of Motya, redolent with ancient grandeur. There in his darkened study were the beautiful inscribed books: Michelangelo's *Love Sonnets and Madrigals to Tommaso de Cavalieri*, front-covered by his *Tityus*.

Hervé Guibert, *To the Friend who did not save my life*, Elie Wiesel's *Night* and *From the Kingdom of Memory*. Seamus Deane *Reading in the Dark*. Primo Levi's *If this is a Man that walked*, and his collection of poems *Ad ora incerta*. There were many, many more, and of course everything by Henry James including the first edition of *Portraits of Places*.

As I ceased to sleep and the dream was slowly fading, a night light burned in the darkness and I heard you singing Solomon's paean to the rising and setting sun.

● ● ●

June 1997
Dear James, - 'with glory and honour'
Congratulations on your CBE. I look forward to your future knighthood.

'In all thy works keep
To thyself the pre-eminence.'

Yours ever,
Maxine

Looking back over a life devoted to music it is clear that everything for James Bowman seems to lose its intensity and interest after a decade. He continues to find new directions; each decade requires a different sound focus. His CBE in 1997 awarded for services to Music, and in October 2000 his appointment as a Gentleman of the Chapel Royal, underlines his position as one of England's elite musicians. The resurgence in James' recorded work is truly wonderful, and includes new commissions. This summer he is playing a leading role in the special celebrations at Handel House, whilst continuing to sing in the choir on Sundays, just as he did as a boy-alto. His membership of the *Athenaeum* gives him access to the finest club library in London. Artistic luminaries and ecclesiastics predominate in a private club that was founded as 'a meeting place for men who enjoy the life of the mind'.

Six Decades
1941   Born in Oxford – Thence to Jesmond, singing as a small boy in St Nicholas' Cathedral.
1950-1965   A decade at Ely, on to Oxford and Westminster Abbey. A sign from heaven.
1966-1976 A decade with Benjamin Britten until his unexpected death in 1976.

1966-1976 A decade with David Munrow before he 'went mad' and died by his own hand. Like Dante's anonymous Florentine suicide in 'The wood of the Grieving Suicides', David Munrow had hanged himself in his own home.

Mid 1980s – 1990s A decade with Robert King before his tragic downfall.

2000 – The Chapel Royal. In the personal service of the Queen, and one of the most important things in his singing life at the moment. Queen Elizabeth I's (Gloriana) celebrated musicians, Thomas Tallis and William Byrd were Gentlemen of the Chapel Royal.

'The Countertenor voice isn't a thing that lasts forever', James Bowman has said, but James has always been an exception to the rule. Many more opportunities and overdue Honours surely await to grace his lifetime, and legacy 'in the gaze of an altered world'.

Arise, Sir James!

• • •

Triple Portrait

Second Study of James Bowman: Britten's chosen Countertenor

James Bowman, portrait by June Mendoza

Like the bright pearl
secreted in darkness,
The baroque Prefaces
and great final novels
of 'The Master of nuance and scruple,'
remain closed to all but a few.
So difficult to enter but impossible to leave.
Cerebral Gloriani in his artist's walled garden.

Milly Theale dreaming of Venice, in love with high places like the Dove she resembles. Turning her face to the wall of her palazzo, when death comes.
Time beats on...

My handwriting is said to closely resemble that of Henry James.
In his poem *At The Grave of Henry James*, Auden wrote 'All will be judged', invoking prayers for all writers, living or dead.

• • •

'He is definitely more moon than sun', observed my lovely mother one august evening in Harrogate, as she watched the solitary James Bowman morosely walking towards his recital venue. I recalled Henry James' phrase 'The solitude of genius'; and knew that they were kindred spirits, both being social and reclusive, and having become fondly acquainted through *The Maxine Handy Library*.
On that hot 3rd August night in 1994 as I sat in the audience, James gave me a charming smile from his elevated arena, before moving ever closer to sing to me. Remote from all others I was an audience of one. Soon after our first meeting in 1992 he had said, 'I think we're very alike, Maxine. We have an empathy.' His profound communication of Purcell songs and Handel arias was both physical and spiritual. I surrendered to the spell he cast:

'At night in dream
a wild dissolving bliss
Over my frame he breathed, approaching near,
And bent his eyes of kindling tenderness
Near mine.'
(Percy Bysshe Shelley)

His erotic charisma resembled that of an archangel, a visitor from an unattainable realm. When Gabriel descends, time and distance cease to exist as god and mortal reverently mingle in what is termed the *annunciation* and *incarnation*.

James' performance concluded, he quickly left the stage and only moments later ran after me to give thanks for the joy of his morning flowers. But I had already gone, just glimpsing his now distant figure as he looked in vain for me outside the Hall. Unseen, I watched him: 'A dream to see', like Hilaire Belloc's 1896 ethereal sphere. But without true-love and knowledge the *Queen of the Night* will disappear into mere memory and never rise again:

'I go where none may understand,
I fade into the nameless land.'
><ins>*The Moon's Funeral*, words by Hilaire Belloc, music by Joseph Phibbs, sung by James Bowman.</ins>

• • •

'He who loves beauty worships me
Mine is the spell that binds his days'

>(The voice of Apollo)

Although worshipped as the radiant, otherworldly and seductive voice of the god Apollo, in Britten's problematic opera *Death in Venice*, ambiguous Oberon in his anarchic wood is James Bowman's true alter ego. Like the God of the Bible in creating and interpreting Adam, he breathed life into Benjamin Britten's King of Shadows. Menacing and spellbinding, sadistic and seductive, Oberon's dark-glinting arias mesmerize with their narcotic, unearthly power. His love-juice upon the eyes is the promise of endless ecstasy and desire. It also acts as death's counterfeit. 'Bowman had lust written all over his lower register', said Peter Hall when directing James in the role at Glyndebourne. Like the winged-Gabriel alighting with his flower in Mary's walled garden, Oberon's love-philtre or fear-philtre invites conquest and submission.

'I love singing Bach. I give it a loving caress, like a velvet glove around the throat.' James Bowman

The following words, spoken to me by James before his performance in Bach's *St Matthew Passion*, are forever treasured, in memory of a *cosa mentale*:

'Maxine! Show me where you're sitting and I'll open my mouth very wide and sing to you...My live performances should leave you in suspended ecstasy, waiting for the next time...They live and then die like a flower, but there should never be any sense of anti-climax.'

(James to Maxine)

• • •

Maurice Sendak, the acclaimed but controversial author of *Where the Wild Things Are*, and *In the Night Kitchen* draws inspiration form artists, musicians and authors. He is quoted as saying 'My gods are Herman Melville, Emily Dickinson, Mozart. I believe in them with all my heart.' He has explained that reading Emily Dickinson's poetry helps him to remain calm in an otherwise hectic and confused world. 'I have a little tiny Emily Dickinson...that I carry in my pocket everywhere.' Likewise, of music, he has said, 'I know that if there's a purpose for life, it was for me to hear Mozart.' Praising Herman Melville's work, he has written 'there's a mystery there, a clue, a nut, a bolt, and if I put it together, I find me.' Sendak's Jewish heritage in combination with a gay sexual orientation led him to conceal and protect his private life. Despite living with his companion, psychoanalyst Eugene Glynn for 50 years before Dr Glynn's death in May 2007, he never told his parents. 'All I wanted was to be straight so my parents could be happy. They never, never, never knew.' Sendak has described the way his work helps him to exorcise childhood traumas. The story of mischievous Max's adventure with the monsters is shadowed with loneliness and melancholy moonlight.

In Alan Bennett's small masterpiece *A Question of Attribution*, Sir Anthony Blunt, intellectual aristocrat and keeper of the Queen's paintings, is an intriguing enigma rather than a crude fake. Thus he resembles the mysterious and haunting painting he is trying to attribute. Formerly, and incorrectly, believed to be a priceless Titian, Sir Anthony and the Queen discuss the Triple Portrait and the complex relationship between a forgery and an Old Master. He points out that the antique painting itself has not attempted to deceive us; it is we the viewers who have misled ourselves.

'Paintings make no claims…They do not purport to be anything other than paintings. It is we the beholders who make claims for them, attribute a picture to this artist or that.'

The exalted surveyor of the Royal Collection continued as adviser to the Queen, despite having spent years as a Soviet spy. Emotionally atrophied and an outsider, Blunt had an appetite for subversion which probably stemmed from his homosexuality, illegal in those days. He lived with his beautiful ex-guardsman partner in an apartment above the Courtauld Institute, but only his inner circle knew about this arrangement. After exposure by Margaret Thatcher, who was determined to destroy him, he became a withdrawn figure, seldom leaving his flat. His anonymity had vanished and he found recognition by the hostile general public to be intolerable. Finally, he attempted suicide by jumping from his balcony, but he survived. A few years after Blunt's death from a heart-attack, his companion left for Scotland and was subsequently killed by a train on an open crossing. The verdict was suicide.

The reasons for the suicide of the early-music pioneer, David Munrow, remain obscure. He was depressive and emotionally complex, and had previously attempted to kill himself by taking an overdose in 1975. But why he chose to hang himself in his own home the following year, is open to speculation. Perhaps his inner conflict and secret-self resembled that of Henry James in Colin Toibin's *The Master*: 'a man whose artistic gifts made his career a triumph but whose private life was haunted by loneliness and longing, and whose sexual identity remained unresolved.'

Perverse courage perhaps, although some believe that grieving suicides do not realise they won't be coming back again to a conscious but transformed afterlife on earth. Recently, a mother and son jumped from the Humber Bridge, to end their torment. Facing east and both dressed in black, the depressed woman holding the hand of her problematic son – their descent into the cold turbulent river was witnessed by a distant spectator. The mother of the boy with fragile-X syndrome surely conceived of death as a cradle, rocking them gently to a new life together, unsullied by their former imperfect selves. A devout wish for transformation had consumed her, the closing waters would effect the longed for metamorphosis.

Just such a melancholy cocoon is inhabited by Handel's childlike, demented hero, Orlando in the opera bearing his name. The part was written for the famous alto-castrato, Senesino. Because the range is the same, Handel's castrati roles provide a huge number of roles for contemporary countertenors. James interprets Orlando as an introspective, other-worldly man of action who descends into a madness born of jealousy and unrequited love. In a profoundly haunting aria he contemplates self-inflicted death, before rescue by a magic narcotic which sends him into a healing sleep:

'Già l'ebro mio ciglio
Quel dolce liquore
Invita a posar.'

Orlando is 'a shade divided' from himself; he suffers a series of visions of The Underworld. With an array of tonal colours Handel shows a complex understanding of Orlando's depression and inner conflict, a cruel mixture of demonic agitation and lethal fatigue. James Bowman described one summer performance of the role, years before at Glyndebourne. Whilst lying on his back on stage singing 'Già l'ebro mio ciglio' he had undergone an ecstatic epiphany, moments which haunted him all evening as he drove home in his car. 'It was like being inside a melancholy cocoon. I loved that.' When James sat beside me either before a recital, or during the interval, I was always aware of his melancholy aura even though he was 'high' on performance. He used to tell me that I was the colour of sunlight, and he the lovely blue.

James has a remarkably sensitive insight into withdrawal and disintegration. He identified Sir Peter Pears, his former teacher and mentor, as having 'a brokenness' after the death of his lifelong companion Benjamin Britten. He described his great friend and colleague David Munrow, with whom he had a decade long pivotal relationship, as having 'gone mad' before his tragic suicide in May 1976. The loss of Britten and Munrow in the same year was a terrible shock to James and resulted in a four year vocal crisis, from which he struggled to recover.

When Orlando loses his mind he thrusts the heroine Anjelica into a cave. 'I often sound insane when I'm singing', James has remarked, and he inscribed my booklet of his *Orlando* recording:

For Maxine –
In her Cave –
James

Orlando is unable to occupy his former identity, like a room with a closed door that is never opened any more. Doing battle with the furies, Orlando recedes further into ghostliness, then through renunciation something shifts slightly in the mind and his painful isolation lessens…

In conversation with James Bowman at his old music club in Hinckley, he told me that he agreed with Henry James on the subject of renunciation. 'Yes, Maxine, we must renounce things!' And on another occasion during a telephone call, I quoted some memorable words by Virginia Woolf in which she expressed her desire 'to be admitted to the warmth and intimacy of another soul.' James was deeply affected by this poignant thought, and he often repeated her words to me, adding that this was what he too wanted. Also, I wrote a short piece for him *on the solace of falling snow*. 'Did it help?' he asked, and promised never to forget it.

Through James Bowman's magnificent association with the Choir of the Chapel Royal, St James's, under Dr Andrew Gant, he has developed a number of interesting new musical collaborations with composers and recital partners, such as Andrew Plant and Joseph Phibbs, the latter being very much of the Britten School. His 2005 recording *Songs for Ariel* revisits his quintessential English repertoire including Purcell's *Sweeter than Roses*, so loved by his great friend David Munrow, and Britten's *I know a bank* from *A Midsummer Night's Dream* 'each track a voyage through a world all its own…a host of pictures from Bowman's life and career' a musical autobiography. This disc excites me as much as his 1988 recording of Vaughan Williams *Blake Songs*, another miraculous interpretation of English Song, and a project close to his heart. The Purcell and Britten on *Songs for Ariel* are especially plangent because returned to after a long absence. Stylistically, the magical aria 'I know a bank' was inspired by Purcell's song of seduction, *Sweeter than Roses*.

James possesses a singing voice with which I uniquely connect; it illuminates my own inner-landscape. His falsetto is produced approximately one octave above his speaking voice and sounds entirely natural, even when coloured by vibrato. The poetic suggestiveness and ease of James' vocal range evoke a Sendakian dreamscape where lonely, imaginative, disruptive children have secret night-time adventures. Mischievous Max longs to be in control and escape to 'Where the Wild Things Are.' The forest in his bedroom resembles Oberon's magic wood. James often said to me, 'You and I are playing.'

As Britten's 'King of Shadows', James Bowman reigns supreme. He has enjoyed a lifelong relationship with the *Dream*: 'Oberon became my alter ego, and I have never felt so at home in any other role.' Oberon both creates and destroys beauty. Tytania's flowery bank is symbolised by the eglantine rose, 'A wound to heal.' The role of the fairy king was originally written for Alfred Deller, one of the early countertenors to emerge as a great soloist. He was unique, but primarily an Elizabethan miniaturist with limited technique for the opera stage. James Bowman recently revealed to Iestyn Davies, about to debut as Oberon, that much of the score was going to be re-written for James, owing to its having been mostly in recitative to accommodate Deller. These changes were intended to make the part 'a bit more adventurous…but then he [Britten] died, which was a bit of a pain!' Iestyn Davis also said that when he approached James to discuss the role, typically he remarked 'Oh don't ask me, it's time for a new interpretation.'

When Henry James lay dying on his couch overlooking the Thames, his thoughts returned to childhood visits to the Louvre's Napoleonic Gallery of Apollo, where as a small boy he had experienced his dream/nightmare. Henry said that his true home was the Galerie d'Apollon. 'Crossing the threshold of the Galerie d'Apollon into the empire of his own creation, was for Henry James the crucial passage of his life and death', said the James scholar Leon Edel. During those final days in London James believed that he was, once more a boy, voyaging to France to meet his brother William in the Louvre. The Hindus say that with its last breath a spirit returns to the place it loves the best, there to remain for one day and night...For Henry, that place was the great gallery of Apollo. Close to its entrance at the head of the staircase, stands the winged Nike of Samothrace, forever expressing the pain of mourning and the triumph of victory. Despite James' acceptance that he cannot forever play the role of Oberon, it will remain his alone in spirit.

Many times James called me 'an exception – a pearl amongst swine'; symbols of transformation were embedded in his epithets. Our friendship was full of sunlight and shadow. Like his vocal transition it expressed, in Byron's words 'all that's best of dark and bright.' Despite the pitch he sounds wholly masculine, with a wonderful eerie coolness to the voice. His singing and his sexual being seemed inextricably mixed into an otherness which defied intrusion; the rites he had established were an elaborate exclusion. In contrast, women's voices at countertenor pitch often sound overly maternal and lacking in sensuality. I loathe the female contralto voice, an aversion which is well documented amongst devotees of the countertenor.

The late Michael Howard, choirmaster at Ely Cathedral in the 1950s when James was a chorister there, was acutely aware that the finest countertenor evolves from the choirboy. Under Howard's regime the sixteen boys developed singing voices that were 'virtually an upward transposition of the true countertenor.' Working with sixteen choristers and eight lay-clerks, he 're-voiced' the choir, insisting on perfect diction and the true Church of England repertoire in the Chapel Royal tradition. 'Services at Ely felt monastic and esoteric. They were as far from populist as it is possible to imagine' writes Peter Giles, countertenor and distinguished author, in his foreword to Howard's autobiographical memoir. Michael Howard worked on ringing consonants, especially the 'r', so characteristic of James. Ely was a vocally demanding place; the natural resonance of the stone vaulted 'quire' was muffled by the wood of the high-canopied stalls. Voices had to be well-developed, and capable of great range and volume to cope with the problematic acoustic.

It was dark – Ely, with its huge booming Nave and miraculous Lady Chapel, that produced James Bowman. Under Howard's guidance he developed his passion for English music, which remains at the heart of his repertoire. 'I come from the English Cathedral Choral background; the English literary and artistic tradition,' James confesses proudly. Despite the freezing winter months and terrible authoritarian school, complete with bullyings and beatings, James found humanity and privacy through the performing of music.

During Michael Howard's 'Elysian days' at Ely he was helped greatly by the wonderful countertenor John Whitworth, and his then assistant organist, Dr Arthur Wills. Each daily service involved repeated ritual but 'the music was re-interpreted for that unique occasion.' James' sensitivity to words in music, their beauty and drama, is part of his Ely heritage, as is perhaps Britten's decision to compose an operatic role for countertenor.

On one occasion the Ely choristers performed at the parish church of Framlingham where Benjamin Britten himself was present. The chamber concert included Britten's canticle *Abraham and Isaac*, hitherto sung by contralto and tenor. On this occasion the part of Isaac was sung by the countertenor, John Whitworth. Michael Howard surmised that his use of the distinctive countertenor timbre in this role perhaps inspired Britten in 1960 to create the countertenor role of Oberon, in *A Midsummer Night's Dream*. 'I wonder if we could have sown the seeds of inspiration.' And of course James went on in 1972 to give the definitive performance of Isaac, with Peter Pears as Abraham, and Britten on piano. It is preserved in BBC archives.

Howard's time at his beloved Cathedral came to an end in July 1958, but the memory of those years remained 'ever green' throughout his life, as lovingly recalled as his childhood holidays on Romney Marsh, spending time with a local shepherd and his dog. This serene companionship was a brief interlude of pleasure away from his terrifying and friendless existence at public school, described as 'like a prison'. This atmosphere in which emotional development is atrophied by being sent away from home when very young, is brilliantly evoked by Doris Lessing in her novel *Love, Again*: 'He was almost certainly sent to a boarding school when he was seven. You know all the dormitories full of little boys calling out for mummy and crying in their sleep…By the time they are ten or eleven, mummy is a stranger.' On more than one occasion James spoke to me of this strange, almost tribal practice of sending young boys to board. Peculiar to the English, he said, and a mystery to those who would never send their children away, because they would miss them too much, and go mad without them.

When Michael Howard resigned he felt like Adam being expelled from Paradise 'for the thought of life without my Cathedral was insupportable.' His assistant organist Dr Arthur Wills was his worthy successor. It was he who taught James Bowman as a senior, and from whom many years later, I commissioned a *scena* to celebrate James 50th birthday in 1991. The piece was composed for the rare medium of solo countertenor and string quartet. Arthur's *scena: A Toccata of Galuppi's* was a marvellous piece, thrillingly performed for the first time on Saturday 24th September 1994 at his music club in Hinckley, where David Munrow had once been President.

For his birthday flowers in November 1997 James requested a bouquet of 'just blue and white in austere juxtaposition.' I wondered at the time if this choice recalled the blue and white rosette worn by the head chorister at Ely, on founders' day. James felt a complete affinity with my listening soul; the origins of our empathy lay in May 1972, long before we met in person. It was his *Songs for Three Voices* recital, broadcast live from London's National Gallery, in aid of the 'save the Titian' fund, which had ultimately given us 'something very beautiful and personal.' James' 1972 early summer recital with Ben Britten and Peter Pears included Britten's Purcell realisation *Sweeter than Roses*, with which I fell instantly in love. The song had originally been a love-offering from Britten to Pears, but he had later transposed it specifically for the voice of James Bowman. Twenty years later, following a journey to Ripon Cathedral on March 2nd 1991, to see James in live performance, I had asked Radio 3 to broadcast the entire *Songs for Three Voices* from their music archives. This they did on the Sunday morning, the day after my visit to Ripon. A young tenor from the cathedral choir said 'he knows he is on the radio tomorrow and is very pleased.' Little did I realise that my chosen concert from May 1972 was in fact a musical highlight of James' career, and one he would never forget: 'To do a concert with Benjamin Britten and Peter Pears was a rare, and wonderful irreplaceable experience, and I'll never forget it…It was one of the great moments in my musical life. I remember it very well. I can remember the whole occasion. I mean it was a dream come true…an honour beyond words.' As he confided to me some years later, after almost ten years of correspondence: 'When things are perfect, Maxine, it is for me just as it is for you, as you describe it.' This was our mutual nirvana.

Pears, was James' voice teacher for a while; 'always the kindly mentor', said James. They shared the belief that music should be made personal and beautiful, like Britten's Schubertian Purcell realisation, *Sweeter than Roses*. 'A voice is a person...each performance should be an act of love,' said Pears. James often quoted these words in describing our own poetical and civilised exchange of performance, response, and correspondence.

'The magic gift of Purcell's with words and music cannot be explained any more than Schubert's can.' (Peter Pears) 'I never realised words could be set with such ingenuity and colour', Britten said of Purcell. Like David Munrow, Britten loved the human voice above all instruments and from 1966-1976 Britten and Munrow dominated the musical life of James Bowman. Yet despite Britten's profound love for the music of Purcell and his understanding of the countertenor's central role in reviving his music, James has always said that it was the conductor Robert King who truly illuminated Purcell.

For James, the approach to words in music was a continuation of his training under Michael Howard for whom music was to be re-created with a strong *personal* input by the performer, so the listener would be spellbound by the music and the power of its rendition. The singer used an emphatic and dramatic attack with *crunching* consonants and *crystal* vowels. After a live performance James would invariably seek reassurance from me on this all important subject: 'Can you hear me, Maxine?' he would ask anxiously. 'It is very difficult to hear sung words in music, especially when singing with modern instruments.' One of his favourite acoustics is the beautiful church of St Martin-in-the-Fields, London. It has a small and intimate performing space which he enjoys. He gave recent recitals there in 2008 and 2009. *The Independent* critic Michael Church found him still sublime 'Where Bowman's one-time pupil Andreas Scholl simply floats his notes, Bowman invests every syllable with urgent meaning; the spell he cast was extraordinary.'

As James has said, all voices darken and acquire more colours with age. In a letter to him I likened this process to the slowly fading tones of an Old Master, which in ageing becomes an ever more beautiful Masterpiece. Now in his sixth decade, the resurgence in James' recorded work expresses this mature genius, overlaid with a deepening melancholy so characteristic of the English sensibility, whether in music or literature. It accords with our exquisite summer rain, radiant autumn colours, and beautiful evergreens in the silvery obscured light of winter.

Many reviewers believe that by the end of 1998 James Bowman's voice was past its best. He himself now acknowledges in 2009 that it is no longer the uniquely expressive clarion call it once was, but that by making a careful choice of repertoire, venue, and partners, it is possible to continue singing. 'I'm a great believer in being a survivor,' he says. 'Countertenor James Bowman employed his ageing voice with vintage artistry,' said a critic on his recent performance in Bach's *St John Passion*. James' art and aesthetic choices were originally shaped by the bleak linear fen-country in which he spent his boyhood. Many great musicians, especially instrumentalists like David Munrow and Robert Spencer have profoundly influenced James and taught him much. Through these remarkable partnerships he has given something unique to every decade; he always finds exactly the right direction to express his ever-developing genius.

In his 2004 recording with the brilliant young Canadian countertenor Daniel Taylor, he poignantly revisits repertoire from his 1960s album, including Dowland's *Flow My Tears*. Again with Daniel Taylor and his Theatre of Early Music, in 2007, he revisits Purcell's *Here Let My Life*, a song which shows Purcell's genius for word-painting and his ability to capture profound human emotion. The text is by Abraham Cowley (1618-1667). James' heartrending performance of this title song is unforgettable:

'Here let my life with as much silence slide
As Time that measures it does glide'

Daniel Taylor, commenting on this disc said: 'To stand beside James Bowman on stage is an honour and to sing with him is a true learning experience; he is a remarkable teacher and musician.'

James magnificent association with the Choir of the Chapel Royal has led to the outstanding 2005 recording of English Church Music: *Music for the Chapel Royal*. Despite leading and igniting the choir since becoming a member in 2000, James retains his anonymity as a gentleman-in-ordinary, a charming example of his humility and patrician reverence for tradition. I love that restraint and reserve; it is so English. Probably the highlight of the recording is his duet with a boy treble, singing Psalm 42 *As Pants the Hart*, which shows 'Handel's unsurpassed human sympathy for the human voice and the human heart.' So says the choirmaster and organist, Andrew Gant.

'Why so full of grief, O my soul:
Why so disquieted within me?'

One of James' most recent discs, the 2007 *Songs of Innocence* again explores the vocal texture of a boy treble and countertenor. The brilliant choirboy is pure innocence, whilst the voice of the legendary countertenor embodies sensuality; it is a thrilling juxtaposition. Said *The Times* in July 2008, 'The voice of experience meets the youth in this album contrasting the voices of countertenor Bowman and the boy chorister Swait. Bowman is the uncle, worldly and artistic, dueting with restraint and phrasing with a characteristic elegance and expressivity that Swait duly and sensibly mimics.' Andrew Swait is a passionate admirer of the great James Bowman, just as Robert King was as a choirboy at St John's Cambridge. Swait, King and Daniel Taylor have all spoken of the overwhelming honour of standing beside him in performance.

When James was singing to me, drawn by what he termed my 'wonderful remoteness from all others', sitting next to me, or kneeling beside me, he became at such moments my winged messenger from a distant dream world: Gabriel descending sublimed through chiaroscuro, just like the twilight atmosphere of Leonardo's *Annunciation*.

Peter Pears was wedded to performance; he carried on working even after a stroke. James once confided to me sadly 'once you retire, you're soon forgotten.' It is not a thought he wishes to dwell on, but he has in the past decade considered his legacy and openly referred to it. To the British Library sound archives he has given a rare recording of himself as boy-treble soloist, and described his legacy thus: 'My greatest contribution to the history of the countertenor voice is the fact that I've recorded a vast amount of music of all period and styles. I'm a great believer in being a survivor...I'm proud of my recorded legacy.'

When I told James of my remarkable vision of him transformed into Leonardo's *The Virgin of the Rocks*, he said 'You see what I am, Maxine.' Several years later he discussed with me his aversion to a conventional biography, saying with distaste 'I don't want a biography Maxine, I don't want people fingering my private life.' He frequently used the phrase 'all this' to refer to *his* work and *my* decade of correspondence, saying with emphasis: 'One day, when I've finished with *all this* I'm going to edit and compile a book from your beautiful letters, Maxine, possibly front-covered by Leonardo's *Virgin of the Rocks*, to be left after my lifetime.' Henry James did just this with the letters of his adoring cousin Minnie Temple, 'wrapping her in the dignity of his art', whilst revealing her absolute love and appreciation of *his* art through a largely one-sided correspondence.

In Henry James late novel *The Wings of the Dove*, Milly Theale (a reincarnation of his dear lost Minnie) is shown by Lord Mark, a striking resemblance between her own face and that of the Bronzino portrait of Lucrezia Panciatichi. By seeing her resemblance to a great work of the past, fading with time, her admirer assimilates her into the world of the Old Master, and bestows on her a kind of immortality. In seeing James Bowman metamorphose into Leonardo's *The Virgin of the Rocks*, I was given a portrait of his voice: a vision of his baritone resonating chamber from which emerges his alto – out of darkness into light, recalling Psalm 27:3.

'You gave much to James, Max' said my friend Peter Giles in 2009. On reading my recently completed second monograph, Peter wrote to me in appreciation: 'It's a *very* interesting read…It's highly revealing and peels a lot of skins away from both of you! I can of course feel the "fading off", not because you state it but because I am aware of it from what you've told me. I shall file this amongst my "literature concerning the countertenor" section.' 8th October 2009.

When at Holy Trinity Church in High Wycombe on Saturday October 18th 1997, I had my vision of James transformed into Leonardo's open triangular composition *The Virgin of the Rocks*, I was sitting close beside him after his world-premiere performance of Geoffrey Burgon's *Merciless Beauty*, a combination of the modern and mediaeval. Leonardo's dark cavern revealing the luminous image within portrays James' vocal transition when singing, his change of life at Oxford when he joined the choirs of New College and Christ Church, and the subsequent life-changing letter from Britten. *On Songs for Ariel*, he movingly performs Edmund Rubbra's *Hymn to the Virgin*. The vocal line declaims the mediaeval text, but clothed in a 20th century idiom.

I find this piece unbearably beautiful and redolent of James' childhood days singing in the Lady Chapel at Ely. He identifies closely with the Christ Child and his mother. James' interpretation of Purcell's *Evening Hymn* is another such masterpiece; on more than one occasion he offered it to me as an encore. Michael White's description of James' performance in Westminster Abbey on November 26th 1995 exactly captures my experience of this song; 'Blue is the colour, Purcell is the name. A very moving affair, not least when James Bowman stood in a small pool of light on the chancel steps and sang into the surrounding darkness – gently, intimately, with a spare and weightless tone – Purcell's ethereal *Evening Hymn*.'

My concluding words must return to *Sweeter than Roses*, said to have bewitched David Munrow, James' great friend and colleague, and ignited their work on English Song: a mutual love. 'My work comes before everything, Maxine. It is much more important to me than people. I cannot respond to or return others feelings for me.' James told me this on Wednesday February 11th 1998 outside the King's Hall in Ilkley, after his 'The Raptured Soul' recital, a mixture of Handel and Purcell. He confided that someone in France was threatening to commit suicide over him, and disturbing his much needed sleep, with nightly telephone calls. This added to James' difficulties at that time, in coping with his dying mother. He said he was under great stress from 'emotional blackmail'.

James is assimilated into the immortality of the glorious Old Masters, fading with time to become an ever more beautiful Masterpiece. In 2010 he has a number of new commissions and recordings, including work with the composer Tarik O'Regan from whom he commissioned *The Appointment*, and a commission from Joseph Phibbs.

In his later years, Benjamin Britten regretted the cruel dismissal of his once close friend W H Auden, and the return of several unopened letters. He felt a remorse of the heart but never acted on it. Alan Bennett's new play at the National Theatre, *The Habit of Art* (2009) imagines a reconciliation between Auden and Britten, masters of words and music respectively, when they are both feeling vulnerable and anguished, each awaiting the storyteller at the Altar of the Dead.

A Question of Interpretation
Time passing...
For ten years I mourned the absence of that voice –
Except for essential research for the purpose of writing my three monographs.
The wounded soul was haunted.
But at night in dreams
The voice still visited –
sometimes cried out...
Disembodied now but eternal
Singing to a finite woman
Alone in a private place
Singled out by his art.
Moving from darkness into light.

'the snow has fallen all is hidden except for the lonely blue sheep.'
Haiku (words and music by "Blaar Kindsdottir"/Colin Matthews. Performed by James Bowman and Andrew Plant, 2008)

• • •

James is leading the choir of sixteen
– Six Gentlemen-in-ordinary and ten boys, the children of the Chapel Royal at St James' Palace. Constituted just as it was in Byrd's day

– Smaller than many Oxbridge Chapels, just room to squeeze into the Stalls. Once Queen Henrietta Maria's personal Chapel
– Now adorned with a couple of pictures from the collection of Elizabeth II and a ceiling by Holbein.

My Triple Portrait is finished, but I rejoice in having limelighted and lived in conjunction with James' genius. Retelling the story three times, revisiting events through repetition and variation has seemed like listening to a *da capo* aria from Handel, sung with minimal ornamentation.

Metamorphosis

Time stands still: John Dowland's (1603) lute song, on the theme of mutability and metamorphosis. Sung to me by James, on many occasions, as a personal encore to his evening performance. 'This is for you, Maxine. Seen through *your* eyes I *am* Leonardo's beautiful Virgin of the Rocks, and yes I agree…but it sounds much lovelier coming from you.'

Time stands still with gazing on her face,
Stand still and gaze for minutes, houres and yeares, to her give place:
All other things shall change, but she remains the same,
Till heavens changed have their course & time hath lost his name.

'Dear Max,
Work on the novelised version you mention…regarding the intriguing and absorbing study of your relationship with JB and his Art…Otherwise you do leave yourself very open to being *misunderstood*…
Love Peter'
Christmas 2009

Addenda: Reflections on a Distant Artist

James Bowman's Last London Recital, 21 May 2011

In sleep he sings to me
In dreams he comes
That voice which cried out to me
And spoke my name

Whilst reading English at the University of Leeds, I fell in love with Henry James. By this time he had of course been dead for many decades, but that made no difference to my passionate, unrequited love for him. Treasured and adored, he lived in the dark of my heart.

Then on May 28th 1972 I heard the singer James Bowman – the greatest countertenor of all time. As I listened to him singing the Britten/Purcell realisation *Sweeter than Roses*, almost Schubertian in its tender beauty, I knew that something uniquely lovely and strange had befallen me: the mystery of attraction. Although two decades were to pass before I met James Bowman in person, and came to know him, those moments of epiphany in 1972 had remained deep within me, to become the foundation of our ten year friendship in the 1990s.

James' early summer concert in 1972, with Britten and Pears, a never to be forgotten musical highlight of his career, and my own deep attraction to the work of Henry James, created a tentative beginning to our empathy and trust. Like the shadowed, enclosed figures in Leonardo's *Virgin of the Rocks*, we enjoyed an innocent and playful communion, surrounded by the dangerous sea. 'We have something beautiful, Maxine, why let others spoil it?' said James in 1998. When singing to me alone during our brief encounters, music was made personal and beautiful. Even after its inevitable end, which brought me so much misery and longing, his special decade remained 'something of our own for ever – to be remembered – '

James' great friend and colleague, David Munrow, had been bewitched by *Sweeter than Roses*. His papers, now deposited at the Royal Academy of Music, contain nothing personal and no key to why 'Munrow died by his own hand at Chesham Bois, Buckinghamshire on 15th May 1976', but they illuminate his obsession with the human voice, especially that of James Bowman. Of all instruments he considered the human voice to occupy a privileged position, thus James Bowman's centrality to Munrow's consort. Instruments were measured against it: 'Wide though it is, the spectrum of sound provided by early instruments can be seen as being made up of different facets of vocal timbre...By 1967, I had the core of the Consort. Then I heard James Bowman and thought that here was the most fabulous "noise" I'd ever heard, so he joined us too.' It is said that James' singing, the voice of a single man, can be heard on the moon, and I like to imagine that this is so. That when the day yields to the night-time and we are covered by sleep, the voice of James Bowman 'extends unbroken beyond the uttermost stars.'

It is not surprising that the Britten/Shakespeare Oberon is referred to by James as his alter ego. Britten's choice of the countertenor voice for the role of Oberon, King of Shadows, gives Oberon a fascinatingly unsettling sound, beyond male and female, a dream-spirit of pure libido. When he describes Tytania's forest bed-bower, his music is bewitchingly sensuous and lush. Oberon's Purcellian *I know a bank*, is one of the most erotic and beautiful arias I have ever heard.

In late 1998 James told me that he was in personal crisis; he was 'wounded and bleeding', being subjected to emotional blackmail, and his invalid mother was dying. He seldom mentioned his family, from whom he had been temporarily estranged after leaving Oxford. His father, Benjamin Thomas Bowman had divorced James' mother, Cecilia Maud Bowman (nee Coote) in 1945 when James was only four years old, and his brother Charles Christopher Benjamin Bowman, just six years of age. Already a pupil at Newcastle Cathedral Choir School, James was packed off as a boarder at Ely, in Festival of Britain year, 1951. In 1950 James' mother had remarried, so by the time he was an Ely chorister he had a stepfather, Mortimer Wilmot Bennitt. However, just two years later, Cecilia and Mortimer were divorced. By the time of his mother's third and final marriage in 1962 to John Ainsworth Gordon, James was a young adult at University. The loneliness and emotional turmoil of his childhood, spent largely unvisited in the authoritarian monastic environment of The King's School, Ely, and the absent father who 'just wasn't interested', profoundly damaged James. The Lady Chapel at Ely Cathedral was inspirational, 'so by my singing am I comforted,' but as James confided to me in 1998, he could not return others' feelings for him. He found it very difficult to trust people, but had a deep need of friends, without whom he would 'probably go insane'. However, his work came before everything; 'It is the most important thing in my life, Maxine. It comes before everything,'

About ten months before his mother's death, James told me that she had planned all the details of her funeral, and that the coffin was to be covered in white snowdrops. Cecilia Maud Gordon died in January 1999 at age 87; it was the right month for snowdrops. I'm sure that James honoured her precise instructions. His mother's family were of Anglo-Irish descent, and from ancient lineage, having given distinguished service in either the Church or the Military. James' great-grandfather, John Baptist Crozier MRIA (1853-1920) was Archbishop of Armagh of the Church of Ireland, and Primate of All Ireland (1911-1920). His only daughter, Alice Maud, who later became the fondly remembered Grandmother of James' early childhood, married Charles Chenevix Coote son of Sir Algernon Charles Plumptre Coote 12th Bt of Ballyfin, County Laois. They had four children, including James' mother Cecilia Maud.

James' great-grandfather, Primate John Baptist Crozier had been a keen horseman. His memory is commemorated on a stained glass window in Armagh Cathedral; also portraits currently hang in The See House Armagh, and Bishops Palace Kilkenny. He died on Sunday 11th April 1920 at the Palace, Armagh and he is buried in the grounds of Armagh Cathedral beside his wife, Alice Isabella.

The family arms:
Shield: - 'Or, on a cross, between four fleur de lys azure, a Crozier of the field.'
Crest: - 'A demi eagle displayed proper, charged on the beast with cross pattee or,'
Motto: - 'Vi et virtute'

● ● ●

David's Lament for Jonathan

Low in thy grave with thee
Happy to lie,
Since there's no greater thing left Love to do:
And to live after thee
Is but to die,
For with but half a soul what can Life do?

So share thy victory
Or else thy grave,
Either to rescue thee or with thee lie:
Ending that life for thee,
That thou didst save,
So Death that sundereth might bring thee more nigh.

Peace, O my stricken lute!
Thy strings are sleeping.

Would that my heart could still
Its bitter weeping

> Poem by Peter Abelard (1079-1142)
> From *The Painted Rose*,
> Michael Howard (1951-rev 1973)
> Dedicated to James Bowman.

Like Ovid, the latin poet Catullus romanised Greek myth and legend. Human passion *in extremis* transforms into an experience of the supernatural and divine, as in the stories of *Bacchus and Ariadne, Peleus and Thetis* (the parents of the hero Achilles): 'born in a golden time before the tribe of gods had gone from the earth.'

In Titian's painting of *Bacchus and Ariadne* the abandoned, bewildered girl watches from the empty beach on Naxos as Theseus' ship vanishes towards the north, heedless of her desolation: 'Voice – colour – and Theseus, all were gone.'

Alone on the island Ariadne continues to gaze at the disappearing hull, searching the water with unflagging grief as a maze of sorrow revolves in her heart. But silhouetted against an expanse of precious ultramarine, the god Bacchus and the human girl, Ariadne, 'pause on a single heartbeat.' Having fallen in love at first sight the god arrives to rescue the forsaken Minoan bride; his companions celebrate amidst discordant music. 'The hand-slap, drum beat, bagpipe, horn and cymbals'. Bacchus has come to console Ariadne, bringing as a wedding present the *Corona* of seven stars, which bears her name. The centaur Chiron, tutor of the young Achilles, brings 'green gifts' from Mount Pelion in honour of life, hope, love, and remembrance.

● ● ●

Just a few weeks ago, in January 2010, I came across a truly remarkable work by the Israeli composer and librettist, Ari Frankel. The 25 minute song-cycle *Wiping Ceramic Tiles* is for solo countertenor with piano or string quartet. I was instantly smitten. In researching the history of the piece I discovered that it had developed from an earlier 50-minute song-cycle for soprano, countertenor, baritone, choir and orchestra, which is itself now being expanded into a 90-minute full-length opera *To Scratch an Angel*, 'containing the impressed history of a master's last hour and - in its forceful brevity – projecting us to the limits of the actual world.'

These several Primo Levi inspired compositions are very closely connected, all sharing the same theme, and central 'wonderful singer…the superlative James Bowman.' The sequence follows a mythic path of a soul's search for kindness and beauty. The angelic figure and MESSENGER who guides PRIMO is sung by James. MESSENGER the guardian angel is sent to the ill and anguished PRIMO to save him from despair. He attempts to comfort and protect him.

<u>Arm Patrol</u>

>As I land on your bed now
>Hold your head in my hand
>There's a breath in your lungs still
>There is time for regret
>
>I don't want you to die now
>But that's why I've been sent
>From the place some call heaven
>The domain of the rest
>
>You are very afraid now
>You are weeping alone

As I fly out the back way
As I go on patrol

(MESSENGER and Cadmus)

Born in Turin, Italy in 1919 and trained as a chemist, Levi joined the anti-Fascist resistance during the Second World War. Captured and deported to Auschwitz in 1944, his survival there and subsequent journey home after liberation by the Russians were the subject of his unforgettable memoirs, and poetry collection *Ad Ora Incerta*. Primo Levi returned to Auschwitz in the spring of 1982, forty years after his imprisonment. A *Sorgenti di Vita* crew went along to document the visit, resulting in an extraordinary interview with Daniel Toaff, the son of the Rabbi of Rome. Levi ended his life in Turin in April 1987.

Ari Frankel has visited Levi's house in Turin and also made a pilgrimage to his grave there, in the city of his birth and death. A web-site devoted to Primo Levi's life and writings has been developed by Frankel, ensuring that interest in this remarkable man will live on and increase, as evinced by his own opera in honour of both the famous writer, detached and intellectual, and the vulnerable tormented soul within.

An earlier version of *To Scratch an Angel* opens in a forest clearing where MUSIC asks MESSENGER to observe and look after PRIMO, and attempt to show him routes to overcome despair, existential depression and other hardships. A safe haven is perhaps HOME:

Home is throats that are seldom sore.
Home is freedom desiring more.
Home is beauty, All is well
I move lightly within my shell
Fly, fly home.
Fly, fly soul.

This questioning, intimate journey clearly recalls Dante; Levi's commitment to memory of so much of *The Divine Comedy* helped him to survive the horrors of the concentration camp. In *Moments of Reprieve* he movingly describes how learning Dante by heart as a young man comes to his aid in *the lager* where he is 'living, but not alive.'

Like the Pilgrim accompanied by his guide Virgil, Frankel's PRIMO has a "deaf duet" with MESSENGER, whom in the early part of the opera he can possibly neither see nor hear. The mental and physical scars of imprisonment in the death-camp never left Primo Levi, for whom MESSENGER is often the voice:

MESSENGER

Touch my wall
Touch my scars
Nobody cares
Nobody dares

Lie with me
Open sea
Nobody plans
Nobody's land

Soft is my fruit
Ripe are my lives
Nobody cares
Nobody dares

The Touch
In frozen empathy I listened to James Bowman singing the excerpts which make up Ari Frankel's 1999 hymnal song-cycle, *Wiping Ceramic Tiles*. It was not until my birthday

celebration on 26th January 2010, in an Edwardian railway carriage with my mother, when we were discussing Frankel's opera, that she reminded me that it was *I* who had introduced James to the writings of Primo Levi. In the early – mid 1990s I had inscribed Levi's memoirs, fiction and poetry, even obtaining a special Italian edition of *Ad Ora Incerta*, and given them all to James to mark his special occasions. He had placed them in what he charmingly and wittily termed *The Maxine Handy Library*. Deeply moved by my gesture he told me that he was taking Levi on holiday with him to Italy, saying 'You have opened my eyes to books, Maxine.'

As I continued to listen to James singing *The Shave*, humanity's mortal search for salvation, I remembered a long ago telephone conversation with James at home: his opening words had been 'Maxine, my face is all covered with shaving foam.' For reasons I cannot fully explain I had found this remark profoundly melancholy and felt deeply protective of him:

The Shave – in which PRIMO sees his image reflected in the bathroom mirror of the childhood house where he was born.

> 'I come with questions, answer not
> I come to hold you in my dark
> ....
> Be my saviour, shave me close.'

James always said that my beautiful letters and cards to him and inscribed books were incorporated into his work. He promised to read everything, including all the Henry James I had sent him. He used to bring my cards to his performances, and often selected an encore inspired by my choice of text. Music chosen to be very personal and beautiful. In the opening passage of Ari Frankel's *To Scratch an Angel*, the composer quotes from many poets including Shakespeare,

Dante, Goethe ('The golden tree of life springs ever green'), Proust, and Federico Garcia Lorca. The quotation form Lorca is from his sleepwalking ballad *Sonambulo*.

'Green, how I love you green…
Green wind. Green branches.'

I had given this poem to James in celebration of his recital, which I was attending. It was inscribed on the card to accompany his flowers for a special occasion. He had adored the Lorca poem, and expressed his feelings on many of our subsequent encounters at live performances.

Verde que te quiero verde.
Verde viento. Verde ramas.

James often discussed with me his love of green as a musical colour, saying , 'You, Maxine, are the colour of sunlight and I the lovely blue. Shall we mingle?' Interestingly, the colour Blue is associated with using the throat in plangent communication and expression, complimented by Yellow, which represents intellect and sacred creativity. Together they produce green, the colour of healing, renewal, forgiveness and unconditional love. Seated beside me during the concert interval at Hinckley's small church, in Vicarage Road, in September 1997, James thanked me for his beautiful yellow-in-blue, morning flowers, sent to brighten his day and commemorate his evening performance. Slowly opening to him, both flowers and literature were devoted to his genius as singer and musician: 'I keep all your letters and books, Maxine. They are very beautiful and safely concealed in the privacy of my study.'

Amongst the seductive literary texts with which Ari Frankel honours Primo Levi and explores eternal violence, is a singular quotation from Marcel Proust. His words form part of the opening lines of the tonal/modal *To Scratch an Angel*, which is about to receive its first performance in Israel.

'They buried him...in the lighted windows, his books arranged three by three kept watch like angels with outspread wings...The true paradises are paradises we have lost.' Marcel Proust, La Prisonni Ure 1,1

• • •

Three is a sacred number in both Christianity and Judaism. The lantern-turret of the synagogue in Hadassah-Hebrew University Medical Centre, is lighted by means of 12 large windows with round arches, three on each side. These sublimely beautiful *Jerusalem Windows* are by the Russian-Jewish artist Marc Chagall, who envisaged the synagogue as 'a crown offered for the Jewish Queen' – the windows as jewels of translucent fire – the vision an echo of the Psalmist's rejoicing. Although, as in Titian's paintings of myths, we are taken into the realm of the supernatural, the Jerusalem windows symbolize the historic twelve tribes of ancient Israel. Their lyric blessings by Jacob and Moses conclude Genesis and Deuteronomy 33:

For they shall suck of the abundance of the seas,
And of treasures hid in the sand.
Moses

The three green windows represent the tribes of Issacher, Gad and Asher, the last being famous for wisdom, beauty, and its fertile hereditary territory. Its principal cultivation was the olive tree, symbol of opulence, joy and light. This area provided oil for the whole land of Israel. Asher's precious stone was aqua-marine with an olive tree drawn on it. This luxuriant window celebrates peace and joy. On the ceremonial table burns the seven-branched menorah, one of the most sacred objects in the sanctuary, the holy of holies. Its perpetual flame was to be maintained with 'pure olive oil beaten for the light.' (Exodus 27:20). This light symbolizes Judaism and has many attributes, both cosmological and mystical. It is represented by the tree of Life, Divine Light, and the glow of planets. The Jews are a light to civilization.

Blue fused with yellow was especially made for the dominant soft-green tonality of the unique tender and calm window of Issacher. In its double thickness it gives green, but the union of two colours makes possible marvellous and subtle transitions from blue to green and to yellow.

James Bowman's glorious dark-blue eyes resemble the beautiful ancestral jewels of Issachor. His spirit in music is akin to the emblem of that exalted tribe dwelling in the green fertile Land of Galilee.

His gem was (SAPIR)
His flag was very dark-blue
His emblem was Sun and Moon, as it is written...
Midrash Rabbah Bamidbar 2

The stage setting for Ari Frankel's chamber opera uses a three-dimensional cut of Levi's family house. At its centre is a wide spiral staircase, hugging an elevator shaft. The PRIMO apartments occupy all of the third floor; the stairwell has a low railing. At the conclusion of Primo's final hour on earth, MESSENGER hovers over his ill, shaking body. As Primo rises and walks uncertainly towards the railing at the top of the stairs, he loses his balance/jumps/slips/and falls over the railing, to his death. After the slow motion , seven minute tumbling fall in which he sees many images, including colours, flowers, and animals, the tableaux fades and goes dark, and we return to real time. There is SILENCE, then there are the last words from PRIMO, fatally injured at the foot of the narrow stairwell, and now completely alone:

Non ne posso piy. I can't go on.

• • •

It is 10:20 am on Saturday April 11, 1987. PRIMO lowers his head, he dies.

Whether or not Primo Levi deliberately ended his life is much debated, although those closest to him think that he did. His son Renzo, who lived in an adjoining apartment, said 'I think my father had already written the last act of his existence. Read the conclusion of *The Truce* and you will understand.' The great writer Elie Wiesel also believed that the horror of Autschwitz was ultimately responsible for Levi's suicide, and Maurice Goldstein, the president of the Auschwitz International Committee, wrote 'Auschwitz reclaimed him.' Also we know that at the time of his death he had been taking anti-depressant medication for several months. His recent operation for prostate trouble had weakened him physically, and the close proximity of his old, senile mother and mother-in-law depleted his ability to continue writing.

Nevertheless, the hypothesis of an accident remains, especially after taking into account his behaviour that final morning. Soon after the concierge's visit to his apartment he re-opened the door and went to the banister. Was he simply looking for the concierge descending the stairs, or did he lean over for the purpose of hurling himself down the stairwell?

Reconstructing the events which surrounded Levi's death can lead to entirely different conclusions: accident or suicide. Ten years after Levi's life ended, the Chief Rabbi of Rome, Elio Toaff, told the academic Diego Gambetta, that Primo Levi had called him on the telephone "ten minutes before" he died.

The Rabbi recalled that Levi sounded distressed, saying, 'I can't go on with this life...' and telling Toaff that he was haunted by the memories of Auschwitz.

However, there are inconsistencies in the Rabbi's account. Levi died on a Saturday; as an observant Jew, it is very unlikely that Elio Toaff would answer the phone on the Jewish Sabbath. Primo always denied any *guru* status for himself, saying that he never cared to draw easy conclusions as he had 'more doubts than convictions.'

Obsidian mirrors, especially those made from the beautiful translucent green variation of the volcanic rock, were used in ancient civilizations for divination. Aztec Shamans used polished obsidian mirrors for *catoptromancy*, a method of divination which interprets patterns and images which might be seen in the mirror. Associated with vision and healing, the divine stone was used to converse with spirits, and diagnose those suffering from 'soul loss', who had therefore become ill. If the image of the person were clear they would soon recover, if shadowy. The soul had been lost. The Royal astrologer and scientific advisor to Elizabeth I, the famous Dr John Dee used just such a sacred stone mirror, hauntingly described by Peter Ackroyd as 'looking at a candle through tears.'

We cherish and remember Primo Levi for his miraculous written pairing of science and atrocity. He relishes every experience of the details of the animate and inanimate world, and of simply being alive as a witness. Ultimately, all is chemistry, elements and compounds. Primo Levi uniquely combines science and mystery to create a terrible, never-ending beauty:

'Better to live in doubt than on an ill-founded certainty.' (Diego Gambetta, Fellow at all Souls College, Oxford). 'Primo Levi's Last Moments.'

• • •

102   *Triple-Portrait of a Countertenor*

Why do I Use My Paper, Ink and Pen?

Why do I use my paper, ink and pen,
And Call my wits to counsel what to say?
Such memories were made for mortal men;

I speak of Saints whose names cannot decay,
An Angel's trump were fitter for to Sound
Their glorious death if such on earth were found.

> Consort song for male high voice and four viols. An epitaph on Edmund Campion, a Jesuit priest who was executed in 1581 and subsequently canonized. Text by the poet Henry Walpole, and set to music by William Byrd.

Afterword

James Bowman and Mahan Esfahani

The Bowman bows out: May 8 2011 by Norman Lebrecht

> 'The outstanding countertenor James Bowman will give his final Wigmore Hall recital on May 21st. I have been listening to him there for half my life and I can't believe I'll never hear him there again, but James is pushing and that's a wise time to go. Oh, my veni, veni, venis long ago...With typical generosity he is sharing his farewell with the fast-rising Iranian-American harpsichordist, Mahan Esfahani. Purcell, Handel and Bach...mmm.'

Comments in reply: Maxine Handy says: May 8, 2011 at 5.40 pm:

> 'I am in entire agreement with your comments. For a decade I attended his every performance, and commissioned a Scena to celebrate his 50th birthday. I have all his recordings and have been listening to his unique voice for over three decades. This year I have at last completed two books on the great James Bowman; they have taken me more than ten years to write but were a labour of love...an offering to this divine artist. Yes, it is sad that he is leaving the London music scene, but James has enjoyed many different stages in his legendary career, and I think that this is just such another. He is not disappearing into memory alone; he will be singing in other, often charming venues. As I have said in my *Triple-Portrait of a Countertenor*, as James slowly fades with time, like an Old-Master, he becomes an ever more beautiful masterpiece.'

● ● ●

James' tender and joyous farewell to his musical life and audiences in the capital celebrated the baroque composers with which he is so closely identified. His chosen repertoire of Handel, Bach and Purcell was a perfect expression of the beauty and vulnerability at the heart of his vocal genius. James took a little while to settle. When he first appeared on stage James admitted to being rather nervous – a touch of stage fright, he said! Some typically mischievous remarks to the audience helped him to relax – he expressed his satisfaction at the wisdom of his public, who had chosen to come to this very special evening at the Wigmore, rather than the abysmal production of *The Dream,* currently on at English National Opera. "Have you read the terrible reviews?" he asked with obvious amusement. "It is set in a boys' prep school. I have had quite enough of those in my life", he added pointedly. Amidst the scornful jokes, it was obvious that James felt much justified satisfaction that this new version of a role with which he had a lifelong identification, was a disaster. James' enchanted bank and magic wood had been replaced by a ghastly boys' school where unprotected children suffered abuse. Reaching for a glass of water to ease his dry throat, James emphasised that he did not want the occasion of his last London recital to be over-emotional, but it was clear that at times during the evening he was overcome, particularly when remembering David Munrow.

The recital brought to a close more than four decades of performance. It was a gentle goodbye, a graceful withdrawal from the Wigmore stage, which he had first stepped upon in 1967 with David Munrow's Early Music Consort. When the veteran Countertenor appeared on the platform, he was greeted with a heartfelt tribute to his supreme artistry. James had invited the brilliant young Iranian-born harpsichordist Mahan Esfahani to join him for his final bow in London, to accompany him, but also to perform solo. It was through a David Munrow recording that Mahan had first encountered

Bowman and the countertenor voice. He produced from his pocket the very cassette he'd bought aged 10 – *Pleasures of the Royal Courts* – and asked Bowman to sign it, tucking the spilling spool back in his pocket as he did so. James highlighted the similarity between the harpsichord and the countertenor – both had started out in accompanying roles, but gradually transformed into solo instruments, which were now taken very seriously. James' decision to share his final London platform was both wise and typically generous. The presence of the thrilling Esfahani gave the evening a fresh excitement and energy, but the spotlight shone firmly on James Bowman. In the first half the capacity audience was treated to Purcell; after the interval James moved to Handel. He delighted us with the exquisite and little known 'Tacerò, pur che fedele' from *Agrippina*, caressed with delicate da-capo ornamentation by James.

Returning to his sole encore, Bowman playfully declined to name it! 'If you don't recognise this one you shouldn't be here'. I knew at once that it would be Purcell's *Evening Hymn*, hailing the setting of the sun. As James closed with the tenderest of legatos, weaving a rainbow tapestry, the audience closed with rapturous applause and a standing ovation.

This last London recital was intended to mark a significant moment in James' career. Although he intends to give recitals elsewhere, he will only perform infrequently. As he approaches his 70th birthday in November, he describes his voice as being 'in reasonably good shape', but in need of conservation. He talks about it as '… a friend – but a friend that can turn on you if it wants to. An alien living in your throat…It has a mind of its own. Quite uncanny.' It is live performance that he will always cherish, and not content with happy memories alone, there are many things still to come. On 25th June at Ely Cathedral he is performing in an evening programme of *Music and Memories*, with works by Tallis, Purcell, Handel, Vaughan Williams and Britten. James will also talk about his professional life and reflect on his time at Ely in the 1950s when he was a chorister. On 1st July 2011 he is singing with Catherine Bott, in an evening recital *A Midsummer Night with Bott and Bowman*, which will include settings of Shakespeare by Britten.

I left the Wigmore Hall with a number of photographs to treasure, including an image of James' final deep bow. As James sings with his entire body he is extremely difficult to photograph; blurred images are the usual outcome. At first I was disappointed by these hazy photographs, until I realised that the phenomenon of the out-of-focus image created its own seductive beauty. 'Unsharpness' presented James in performance as being in a state 'between apparition and dissolution between memory and forgetting'. Upon my return home I had the photographs professionally adjusted; an intricate process during which the boundaries between painting and photography were themselves blurred. This resulted in a complex and dynamic instability, which was at the heart of James' vocal agility in live performance. I felt that through these portraits his spirit was made visible and free.

James Bowman's final bow

Coda – A very special painting, May 2004

'One paints a thing in order to know it, see it.'
Dorothy Bradford

It was as a painter of musicians in performance that Dorothy Bradford made her unique contribution to art. She preferred to draw at rehearsals, where the repetition of musical passages and musicians gestures enabled her to define individual characteristics. "Music needs time and repetition to get the sense of the thing as a whole". Her fluid, energetic brushwork and minimal colour relationships express the individual gestures of hands, posture, sounds and emotion specific to that event. "In a painting I need to sing".

The outstanding musicians portrayed by Dorothy Bradford included countertenor James Bowman; indeed his portrait is one of her best known and most important works. At her memorial service the huge painting of James singing in St Oswald's Church, Worleston, in May 2003 was placed on the wall behind the pulpit. Bodies in movement fascinated Dorothy, and James sings with his entire body, from the feet upwards – so a perfect subject. The portrait captures exactly, in a wonderful palette of blues orange and yellows, James Bowman the social and solitary being. And like the famous countertenor himself, she communicates the power of what persists in the silence after the reverberations of sounds have concluded. "The music remains in the air like an after-image on the retina".

James Bowman
Complete Discography

Compact Discs

J S Bach	B Minor Mass	Collins 70322
	Solo Cantatas	Hyperion CDA66326
	St Matthew Passion	Teldec 2292-42509-2
	St John Passion	Philips 434 905-2
Biber	Requiem	Ricercar RIC081063
Blow	Ode on the death of Mr Henry Purcell	RCA Victor D134250
Britten	Midsummer Night's Dream	Virgin Classics VCD7 59305-2
	Death in Venice	London 425 669-2LH2
	Canticles	London 425 716-2LM
	Rejoice in the lamb	EMI CDM5 65111-2
	Purcell realizations	Hyperion CDA67061/2
Bruhns	Complete cantatas	Ricercar REC 8001/2
Burgon	Fall of Lucifer	Silva Classics SILKD6002
	Canciones del Alma	EMI CDC7 49762 2 or EMI CDM 5 66527 2
	Merciless beauty	ASV Classics CD DCA 1059
Buxtehude	German baroque cantatas vol 7	Ricercar RIC094076
Byrd	Consort songs, English Consort Music (I)	Ricercar RIC206442
David Cain	Play music by David Cain	BBC Records ZBBC 1925
Campian etc.	Elizabethan ayres and dances	Saga EC 3354-2

Triple-Portrait of a Countertenor

Cavalli	Calisto	Decca 436216-2DM02
Charpentier	Messe de minuit	EMI CDM7 63135-2
Couperin	Lecon de ténèbres	Hyperion CDA66474
Dowland	Lute Songs	Hyperion CDA66447
	Lute songs	Saga EC 3375-2
Dufay	Missa Se la face ay pale	Virgin Veritas 61283
Du Mont	Motets a deux voix	Ricercar RIC068053
Early Music Consort	Art of the Netherlands	EMI reflexe 64215
	The Medieval Experience	DG Archiv 449 082 2
	Monteverdi's contemporaries	Virgin Veritas 61288
	Art of courtly love	Virgin Veritas 61284
	Music of the gothic era	DG Archiv 415 292
	Music of the gothic era (2 CD's)	DG Archiv Produktion "Codex" 453 185-2
	Gregorian Chant, Perotin & Machaut	DG Archiv 4439 424-2
	Music of the crusades	Decca 430 264-2
	Ecco la primavera	Decca 436 219
	The pleasures of the royal courts	Nonsuch 71326
	The Triumphs of Maximilian I	Decca Serenata 436 998
	Adieu Madame - Music at the English Court	Deutsche Harmonia Mundi GD77 178
Gabrieli	Christmas motets	Hyperion CDA66398
Grier	12 Anthems	Herald HAVPCD177
Gluck	Orfeo ed Euridice	Astree E 8538
Handel	Admeto	Virgin Veritas 5 61369 2
	Ariodante	Phillips 442 096-2
	Athalia	L'Oiseau Lyre 417 126-

		2
	Belshazzar	Archiv 431 793-2
	Chandos anthems vol 3	Chandos CHAN0505
	Deborah	Hyperion CDA66841/2
	Giulio Cesare	Astree E 8558
	Julius Caesar	EMI CDMS7 69760-2
	Israel in Egypt	Decca 443 470-2DF2
	Joshua	Hyperion CDA66461/2
	Joseph & His Brethren	Hyperion CDA67171/3
	Judas Maccabaeus	Hyperion CDA66641/2
	Messiah	Erato 2292 45960-2 or Erato ECD 880503 or Erato 0630-17766-2
	Messiah	EMI CMS5 63784-2
	Messiah	EMI CDS7 49801-2
	Messiah	Pro Arte CDD 232
	Music for royal occassions	Hyperion CDA66635
	Foundling hospital anthem	L'Oiseau Lyre 421 654-2OH
	Occasional Oratorio	Hyperion CDA66961/2
	Orlando	L'Oiseau Lyre 430 845-2
	Ottone	Hyperion CDA66751/3
	Saul	Archiv 447 696-2
	Silla	Somm SOMMCD 227-8
	English Arias	Hyperion CDA66483
	Heroic Arias	Hyperion CDA66797
	Italian Duets	Hyperion CDA66440
	Tercentenary Concert	BBC Radio Classics

Herbert Howells	Full moon and O my deir hert	15656 91522 Meridian CDE84158
Kerll	Missa pro defunctis	Ricercar RIC081063
Johann Kuhnau	Sacred Music	Hyperion CDA67059
Loussier	Messa Baroque du 21 Siècle	Decca 425 217-2 or Media 7 M7 856
Monteverdi	L'Incoronazione de Poppea	Virgin Veritas VCT5 45082-2
	L'Orfeo	Archiv 447 703-2AX2
	Vespro della Beata Virgine	Decca 443 482-2
Nyman	Time will pronounce	Argo 440 282-2ZH
Orff	Carmina Burana	Decca 444 591-2 or Decca 411 702-2
	Carmina Burana	Virgin Classics CUV 5 61262 2
Palestrina	Canticum Canticorum Salomonis	Hyperion CDA66733
Pergolesi	Stabat Mater	L'Oiseau Lyre 425 692-2
	Salve Regina	Meridian CDE84327
Praetorius	Dances from Terpsichore & Motets	Virgin Veritas 61289 2 7
Henry Purcell	Odes and Welcome Songs vol 1	Hyperion CDA66314
	Odes and Welcome Songs vol 2	Hyperion CDA66349
	Odes and Welcome Songs vol 3	Hyperion CDA66412

	Odes and Welcome Songs vol 4	Hyperion CDA66456
	Odes and Welcome Songs vol 5	Hyperion CDA66476
	Odes and Welcome Songs vol 6	Hyperion CDA66494
	Odes and Welcome Songs vol 7	Hyperion CDA66587
	Odes and Welcome Songs vol 8	Hyperion CDA66598
	Three Queen Mary odes	Virgin Veritas VC7 59243 2
	Birthday Ode for Queen Mary (1692 & 1694)	EMI Eminence CD-EMX 2134
	Queen Mary ode, Funeral Music & Organ Works	EMI Classics "Rouge et Noir" CZS 767 524-2 or EMI Classics 7243 5 69270 2 5
	Anthems and Services vol 1	Hyperion CDA66585
	Anthems and Services vol 2	Hyperion CDA66609
	Anthems and Services vol 3	Hyperion CDA66623
	Anthems and Services vol 4	Hyperion CDA66644
	Anthems and Services vol 5	Hyperion CDA66656
	Anthems and Services vol 6	Hyperion CDA66663
	Anthems and Services vol 7	Hyperion CDA66677

	Anthems and Services vol 8	Hyperion CDA66686
	Anthems and Services vol 9	Hyperion CDA66693
	Anthems and Services vol 10	Hyperion CDA66707
	Anthems and Services vol 11	Hyperion CDA66716
	Anthems, Instrumental music and Songs	Teldec 9032 77608 2
	Te deum & Jubilate & Funeral music	Decca 430 263-2DM
	Secular Songs vol 1	Hyperion CDA66710
	Secular Songs vol 2	Hyperion CDA66720
	Secular Songs vol 3	Hyperion CDA66750
	Complete Theatre music (6 discs)	L'Oiseau Lyre 425 893-2
	Mr Henry Purcell's most admirable composures	Hyperion CDA66288
	Countertenor duets and solos	Hyperion CDA66253
	Vocal works	EMI CZS7 67524-2
	Dioclesian acts 1 – 4	Chandos CHAN0568
	Dioclesian masques & Timon of Athens	Chandos CHAN0558
	Dido & Aeneas	Chandos CHAN0586
	The Fairy Queen	Decca 433 163-2DM2
Alan Ridout	Epitaph for Amy Three sonnets of Cecil Day Lewis	Meridian CDE84158
Betty Roe	The Music Tree	Somm SOMMCD 208

Scarlatti & Hasse	Salve Regina	Hyperion CDA66875
Schütz	Symphoniae Sacrae	Chandos CHAN0566/7
Tavener	Akathist of Thanksgiving	Sony SK64446
Telemann	Cantatas	Meridian CDE84159
Various	Ikon	Hyperion CDA66928
	Great baroque arias pt 1	Allegro PCD 894 or MCA Classics MCAD-25213
	Baroque choral & string works	Arion ARN68026
	Italian cantatas	Arion ARN68046
	Recital	Meridian CDE84126
	Baroque vocal works	Meridian CDE84138
	Music from the Courts of Europe - London	United 88002 or Cala 88002-2
	German baroque cantatas vol 6	Ricercar RIC079061
	German baroque cantatas vol 8	Ricercar RIC103086/87
	Solo Alto Cantatas	Ricercar RIC101095
	Lo Sposalizio	Hyperion CDA67048
Vaughan Williams	Ten Blake Songs Linden Lea and other songs	Meridian CDE84158
Vivaldi	Sacred music vol 2	Hyperion CDA66779
	Stabat Mater & Nisi Dominus	L'Oiseau Lyre 414 329-2OM
	Nisi Dominus	L'Oiseau Lyre 443 199-2OM
	Nisi Dominus	L'Oiseau Lyre Double

			Decca 455 727-2
		Vespers for the nativity of the Virgin	Astree E8520
	Peter Warlock	My own country and other songs	Meridian CDE84158
	Weckman	Complete Cantatas	Ricercar RIC109097/098
	Compilations	Baroque beauties	Carlton ORCD11010
		Discover the classics – heroes & heroines	Carlton PCD894 or Pickwick PCD58
		Discover the classics - set 1	Pickwick BOXD21
		These you have loved Vol. 3	Classics for Pleasure CD-CFP4332
		Sacred Music	EMI EG764263-4
		Recital	EMI France 4 83086 2
		The Bach Family	Ricercar RIC92001
		The Music of the Kings Consort	Hyperion king1
		Essential Purcell	Hyperion king2
		The James Bowman collection	Hyperion king3
		The Kings Consort Baroque collection	Hyperion king4
		Portrait	Decca 436 799-2
		The world of sacred music	Decca 436 404-2DW0
		The world of Henry Purcell	Decca 443 393-2DW0
		The glory of Purcell	L'Oiseau Lyre 444 629-2OH

	England, my England (Film soundtrack)	Erato 0630 10700-2
	Le temps des Castrats	EMI CDC 5 55054-2
	La musique au temps des Castrats	Astree E8552
	Les Festes Champestres	Astree E 8631
	Fairest Isle	BBC Music Magazine BM 1
	The art of James Bowman	Meridian CDE 84332
	Intimate Baroque	Summit 118
	If music be the food of love	IMP 6801052

LPs

J S Bach	St Matthew Passion	Telefunken SAWT 9572/75
Bernstein	Chichester Psalms	EMI ASD 3035
Blow	Ode on the death of Mr Henry Purcell	Phillips 6575016
Britten	Rejoice in the lamb	EMI ASD 3035
	Canticle 2	EMI CSD 3772
	Canticle 4	Decca SXL 6608
	Death in Venice	Decca set 581-3
Byrd	Ceremonial Tudor church music	Argo ZRG 659
	Music of the English home	Turnabout TV 34709
Campian etc.	Elizabethan ayres and dances	Saga (number unknown)
Cavalli	Calisto	Argo ZNF 11/12

Charpentier	Messe de minuit	EMI S-36528
Desprez	Missa "L'Homme Armé"	Archiv 2533 360
Dowland	Lute songs	Saga 5449
Dufay	Missa Se la face ay pale	HMV CSD 3751
	Motets	Archive 2533291
Dunstable	Motets	Archive 2533291
Early Music Consort	Art of the Netherlands	EMI SLS 5049
	Art of courtly love	HMV SLS 863
	Music of the gothic era	DG Archiv Produktion 2710 019
	Music of the crusades	Argo ZRG 673
	Music of the Royal Courts of Europe 1150-1600	World Record Club ST 1108
	Henry VIII and his six wives	HMV CSD A9001
	The Art of the Recorder	EMI SLS 5022
	Monteverdi's Contemporaries	HMV SQ ASD 3393
	Love, lust, piety and politics Music of the English court from King Henry V to VIII	BASF/Harmonia mundi 25 22 286-1
	Elizabeth R - Theme and Incidental Music and song	BBC Records RESL 4
	Play music by David Cain	BBC Records REC 91S
	Ecco la primavera	Argo ZRG 642
	The Triumphs of Maximilian I	Argo ZRG 728
	Music for Ferdinand and Isabella of Spain	HMV CSD 3738

	Renaissance Suite (from the film "La course en tête")	HMV HQS 1415
Gretchaninov	Russian Creed Featured in "World of Your Hundred Best Tunes" series also "100 Greatest Classics" volume 3	TRX 103
Handel	Admeto	EMI IC 163-31 808/12
	Athalia	L'Oiseau Lyre 417 126-1
	The Choice of Hercules	EMI ASD 3148
	Julius Caesar	EMI EX-2702325
Di Lasso	Penetential Psalms	Archiv 2533 290
Machaut	La Messe de Nostra Dame	Archiv SAWT 9566-B
Monteverdi	Vespro della Beata Virgine	Decca SET 593040
	Selva Morale E Spirituale	Amadeus AMS 011-12
	L'Orfeo	Archiv 2723 018
Morales	Magnificat and Motets	Archiv 2533 321
Ockeghem	Requiem Mass	Archiv 2533 145
Praetorius	Dances from Terpsichore & Motets	HMV CSD 3761
Purcell	Birthday Ode for Queen Mary (1692 & 1694)	EMI/HMV ASD 3166
	Sacred Music at the English Court	Telefunken SAWT 9558-B
	The Fairy Queen	Decca SET 499-500
	Come, ye sons of art	Musicmasters MM 20005

	Ceremonial Music	Argo ZRG 724
Schütz	Voices and Brass	Argo ZRG 576
	Musikalische Exequien	EMI 065-03 828
	Christmas story	Argo ZRG 671
Tavener	Canciones Espanolas	RCA LRL1 5104
Vivaldi	Stabat Mater & Nisi Dominus	L'Oiseau-Lyre DSLO 506
Various	Songs in Shakespeare's plays	Archiv 2533 407
	Elizabethan lute songs	EMI HQS 1281 or EMI Eminence EMX2101
	Music from the 13th Century	Harmonia Mundi HMU 443
	Sacred music from the 15th/16th Centuries	Archiv 2533 361
	Anthems for the Chapel Royal	Argo ZRG 855
	The King's Musick	EMI C 063-30 119
	Motets by Monteverdi, Gabrieli & Schütz	L'Oiseau-Lyre SOL 333
	Christmas music	Abbey Records ABY 603
	Fantasies, Ayres & Dances	Rosetree RT 101

Videos

Britten	Death in Venice	(number unknown)
	Midsummer Night's Dream	Castle CV12008

Handel	Giulio Cesare	MCEG VVD383	
	Honour, Profit, Preasure	1984 Number unknown	
Soundtrack	Elizabeth R. part 4	BBC Video BBCV5641	
Soundtrack	Zardoz	CBS/FOX No. 1298	
Soundtrack	Rhapsody in August	A Kurosawa film Number unknown	
Soundtrack	A corps perdu	Canadian film by Léa Pool Number unknown	

Printed in Great Britain
by Amazon.co.uk, Ltd.,
Marston Gate.